My Encounters
with Jesus and His Angels

As experienced by
Apostle ATB Williams

UK ⟨signature⟩ 27-07-17

Revival House Publishing UK

My Encounters with Jesus and His Angels

Published by Revival House Publishing
56-62 New Cross Road,
London SE14 5BD

Printed in the United Kingdom.

A CIP Catalogue record for this book is available from the British Library

ISBN 978-1-908592-00-2

Printed by and bound in Great Britain by
www.designxpirit.com
02080901776
© Inside Art illustration

Revival House Publishing UK
www.revivalhousepublishing.com
0208 133 9362

ACKNOWLEDGEMENTS

I thank God the Father of our Lord Jesus Christ for the privilege of knowing Him, and my Lord and Saviour Jesus Christ who also appeared unto me and gave me the opportunity of all my encounters and in-depth revelations of my heavenly encounters.

My first and special appreciation goes to my Mum and Dad, Elder Alfred Osorinwale and Mrs Comfort Olasunmibo Williams. From a very tender age they told me about the prophecies spoken by the founding fathers of (C.A.C) Christ Apostolic Church before I was conceived concerning my calling and Apostleship. This inspired me to join the prayer band of the same church where I was born and raised.

I cannot but also thank my spiritual mother, Madam, Feyisetan (Mama Ketu), (a great prophetess of our age and a seer) who prophesied about my birth, and also lived to see the beginning of the manifestation.

My appreciation goes to Pastor Don Bishop of the Olivet Deptford Baptist Church who recognized the call of God upon my life. He appointed me as his associate pastor in 1984 and recommended me to the F.I.E.C (Fellowship of Independent

Evangelical Churches UK) which led to my first ordination Reverend in 1985.

Although all the aforementioned saints have gone to glory, yet the legacy of the knowledge of the true God they imbedded in me, lives on.

Thanks to Apostle Ulyses Tuff, a co-labourer in His vineyard, and the entire leadership of, "The Way, The Truth and The Life Church", who officially recognised the gift of apostleship in my life and ordained me as an apostle on the 18th December 1996.

I appreciate Prophet Robin Hancox for his continuous support and encouragement to me during these long years we have toiled together in His Vineyard.

What would I have done without the support of the leadership and the entire members of Christ Faith Tabernacle Church globally over the years? You are awesome people! It is my pleasure to serve God through you all. Thank you.

Special thanks to my editorial team: Deaconess Josephine Imonikhe, Pastor Cornelius Ajayi, Deacon Steve Chukwu, Brother Samuel Olomo, Brother Godslove Chinekwe, Sister Pamela Chinekwe, Dr. Nkongho Arrey-Ndip, Sister Toyin Sogbesan and Commision plus, who have taken it upon themselves to work day and night to assist in editing and publishing this book. Thank you Sister Ade Adeyemi, for the initial prompt towards this project.

Special thanks to my Children who have coped with me during these period s of my encounters with Jesus and His holy angels; even when they did not fully understand what I was going through at the time I have had to answer the call of God while they missed my presence.

My profound appreciation goes to my beautiful and amicable wife, Reverend Oma Williams, for her unflinching support for me during the awesome thirty eight years that we have loved one another.

May the deep prophetic power, from God the Father rest upon everyone who reads this book.

PRAYER

Father, I thank You for the grace bestowed on all mankind to know the only true God.

Lord, I ask that Your Holy Spirit will open the understanding of everyone reading this book to know You better.

I also pray that as they read and meditate on the contents of this book, they may encounter Your presence, Your majesty and glory, in Jesus' Holy name, **Amen.**

CONTENTS

God will keep revealing
Himself to many in this
generation...if only they
seek Him.

Apostle ATB Williams

INTRODUCTION

*A*s I travel from nation to nation, the Lord reveals Himself through me in spectacular ways. He sometimes gives me specific revelations and prophecies for those nations. Each time I share my experiences and encounters, the hearts of listeners get stirred up. Hence the collation of the contents of this book is aimed at providing each reader with an unambiguous account of how I got to the point where visiting heaven, having conversations with God the Father and Our Lord and Saviour Jesus Christ, receiving direct instructions from the Holy Spirit and angelic visitations, became a regular occurrence. I believe every Christian can encounter God as highlighted in the scriptures. I would very much want to place emphasis on the phrase every Christian, that is not only those in positions of authority in the church. An example is the story of the prophet Samuel, who heard God's audible voice at a very tender age as written in *1 Samuel 3: 10*. The Bible also talks about prophets like Jeremiah and Isaiah, who were among the four 'major' prophets that existed in the Old Testament. These prophets, in their era, were notable spokesmen for God who made known His word and will to His people.

They had tremendous encounters with God and I know from my personal experience that, in our very own era, it is possible for a mortal man to be taken to heaven and have a glimpse of his eternal home while still alive. If heaven is your home and final destination, would you not want to see your ultimate resting place before you die? There is nothing wrong with the desire to have your own glimpse of where you will spend eternity.

On earth today, just as it was in biblical days, there are people who have developed a good relationship with God; hence He reveals to them mysteries. Sometimes, He reveals the hidden agenda of mankind and demonic spirits, and also His global plans to such people. I happen to be one of those who have had the privilege. I consistently have angelic visitations and God has accorded me the privilege of visiting heaven several times. Jesus Christ has also appeared to me, time and time again.

Deuteronomy 29: 29 (NIV) says:

"29 The secret things belong to the Lord our God, but the things revealed belong to us and our children for ever, that we may follow all the words of this law."

Also, *Amos 3:7* says:

"7 Surely the Sovereign Lord does nothing without revealing His plan to His servants the prophets."

The frequency with which my heavenly encounters occur is such that if I do not see Jesus or have a visitation of heaven in a year, I start getting worried and subsequently begin praying earnestly for it. Often, before that year runs out, or at the latest in the new year, I receive a visitation. All the things the Lord tells me happen exactly as He reveals them.

The Lord has taken me to heaven on several occasions and these experiences are shared as an attestation to the Glory of God. The Holy Spirit is our guide and He will guide us into all truth. It is out of my earnest desire for God that these encounters manifested in my life. My sincere desire for you as a reader is that your yearning for God will bring you to the place of seeking Him regularly so that you may encounter Him the same way.

*C*all unto me, and I will answer thee, and show thee great and mighty things, which thou knowest not.'

Jeremiah 33:3 (KJV)

1

WHO IS THE MAN?

APOSTLE ALFRED THEOPHILUS BABATUNDE WILLIAMS

*B*efore my calling into full-time ministry, I was a land surveyor by profession. Following my involvement in television broadcasting, I went to study for an honours degree in Multimedia Arts majoring in Television Broadcasting. I also hold certificates in Bricklaying and Sound Engineering, which I studied to encourage and help in teaching those who are not academically inclined. *(See my book The Call of an Apostle for more details about my professional endeavours)*

The beginning

My mother was barren for thirteen years and I was the second child and the first son of her marriage. Before my conception and subsequent birth, my father had been a Spiritist and a Chief Priest of Satan, extremely involved in the knowledge and practice of occultism. There was a point in time, within the demonic realm, when he had met and communicated with the demons that operated with Hitler during the Second World War. He had gone to meet with some of his demonic friends (evil spirits) and discovered that most of them were not available. He enquired about their whereabouts from the demon in charge of the relevant information and was told that they had gone to Germany to join one of their counterparts, a fellow member of the occult, in fighting a battle. My father curiously asked what the name of that person was and the demons replied, 'Adolf Hitler'. They elaborated that Adolf Hitler had a mandate to eradicate all Jews and Christians. To this day, anyone seeking to kill Christians and Jews is instigated by the same spirits that propelled Hitler. I am very confident that no individual or group of people will be able to achieve this, not as long as the God who created the heavens and earth lives.

While I was a pastor at Olivet Deptford Baptist Church, in 1984, I shared this with some members who found it hard to believe until a few years later when this was confirmed in a documentary on a major television station in the UK.

The purpose for narrating my father's interaction with the demons that worked with Hitler is to further highlight the depth of occultism my father had been involved in before my conception. For a long time Satan had deceived my father that he was the Almighty God, until my father married my mother who was a priestess of Baal but barren. My father, having practised occultism himself and being involved in helping barren women to conceive, failed in getting my mother a child; hence he invoked Satan who told him that he could not help him on this occasion. It was in this encounter that Satan told my father about the true God and led my father to Christ Apostolic Church (CAC), Ebute Elefun, Lagos, Nigeria.

Unknown to my father, at that time God had raised a man called Apostle Joseph Ayo Babalola and some other renowned men and women of God who worked alongside him. Apostle Joseph Ayo Babalola was the first indigenous apostle raised by Jesus Christ in the African continent. He was called by the Lord in 1927, and held his first major crusade in 1930. He pioneered a movement which birthed the CAC of Nigeria. It was in this church that my parents gave their lives to Christ *(A full account of my father's conversion can be found in my book The Call of an Apostle).*

My mother's conversion was no less a divine occurrence, that is taking her background into consideration. My mother was the daughter of a Chief Imam (a Muslim cleric) in a village called Abule Ifo, near Abeokuta, Ogun State in Nigeria, and she was also a priestess of Baal. After my parents' conversion to Christianity, Apostle Babalola and some other prophets informed my father that the reason for my mother's inability to conceive was because his first son would be an apostle sent to England and would be based in London; hence the Lord could not permit his birth while they were still worshipping the devil. Isn't that wonderful? God saved my parents because of me! For if I had been born at the time my parents were serving the devil, the mandate of God upon my life would not have been fulfilled; therefore, God allowed my conception after my parents' conversion so that they could guide me in the way of the Lord. My parents received a lot of prophecies concerning my life, including being told I would be an apostle of God sent to Europe but based in the United Kingdom (UK) and that I would be a catalyst for the great revival that would occur in the UK. They received the prophecies, every one of them, with a heart of thanksgiving and great anticipation and vowed that they would release their son to God if God gave them one. The reason behind that statement was because, in some parts of Africa, there is a cultural concept which requires every first son to be dedicated to serve either the true God or some other deity, depending on which one a family or clan believes in.

My childhood

As I was growing up, my parents informed me that at the tender age of three, they observed that I spent most of my time praying and behaving distinctively, to the extent that when kids around me were fighting, cursing and abusing one another, my response was always to bless them. For example, if a child called me 'stupid' I would respond, 'You are not stupid in Jesus name.' These unusual responses and behaviour formed my personality as I grew up. If anyone spoke to me in a negative way, I would always respond positively.

By the age of nine, I had joined an intercessory group in Nigeria called Light of the World. They were one of the most renowned intercessory groups in Nigeria, being the praying arm of Christ Apostolic Church. I was the youngest member of the group in the whole of Nigeria during my tenure there. It was in this group that I got established in the act of praying and living a godly life.

The Lord revealed a lot of things to me while I was growing up. It was through this intercessory group that I got involved in various outreaches and crusades, especially to the idol worshippers, which developed my strength, courage and great confidence in God. I was involved in ministering to the sick and the first dead person that was raised to life in my ministry was while I was a teenager.

If you make up your mind to adopt a godly lifestyle (according to the scriptures) and emulate some of the spiritual principles I have practised and found effective, as written in this book, for at least 30 days, you will most certainly have fresh encounters with God and experience a tremendous positive change in your life.

" There was a time He appeared to me in a human figure wrapped in a cloud. You could see the human form but surrounding Him was endless cloud... **"**

" The strong beam that emanated from Him is beyond description. I opened my mouth to try and ask Him for power but I could not utter a word... **"**

"... then Jesus took my right hand and said, 'let's go'... **"**

"I instantly saw my spirit depart from my physical body as we both began to glide through clouds into clouds. The exhilarating sensation of this form of travel is totally amazing. The best way I can describe it is that it is like travelling in a see-through aeroplane at a much faster speed..."

“...He left me with the words again, “Go now and start the work”. His departure was as sudden as His arrival, as abruptly the wall of my room began to close up once more while He disappeared into the clouds...”

2

THE CALL TO MINISTER

*D*uring my teenage years, I was determined not to become a pastor, despite all the prophecies spoken about me. This was because, at that time, all the pastors I knew endured a lot of negligence at the hands of their members and were not properly cared for by their churches. I observed that while church members were constantly demanding their pastors' time and attention, nevertheless, they had a nonchalant attitude towards the personal needs/welfare of their pastors. Those who were the most opposed to contributing towards the comfort of their pastor were sometimes the most wealthy and influential in the church and community. They felt it was a luxury for their shepherd to own a vehicle and, therefore, preferred him riding a bicycle to visit members in their homes or in hospital. They cared little for the comfort of their pastor who laboured day and night before God in prayer and supplication concerning their spiritual and personal well-being. They ignored the fact that his persistent prayers and supplication before God were instrumental to the physical manifestations of goodwill taking place in their lives.

Back then, ministers and pastors were subjected to unnecessary punishments and hardship by the church. Having always been passionate about my independence, I decided that I was not going to be subjected to the control of a person or groups of people who supposedly would determine what salary and benefits I was entitled to. I preferred, rather, to use my intellect to gather wealth and definitely be the sole determiner of how much I earned and the comfort I enjoyed. I was therefore certain that I could earn as much as I wanted. Since my best subjects were Mathematics and Physics, I decided to further equip myself with more knowledge by studying Land Surveying and Mapping Sciences.

As a land surveyor, my greatest desire and intention was to sponsor those who had the desire to preach. I also had an ambition to become the first African surveyor to own companies in the western world. From my time at George Wimpey International in 1979, I figured that if someone from England could start a multi-million pound company in Africa, I could do likewise in Europe. It became one of my driving forces and ambitions in life to become a trailblazer. I had an understanding that God was going to start an institution through me in the UK, spreading across Europe to the rest of the world, but what I never understood was that it would happen through the spiritual mandate upon my life. I thought my physical power, knowledge and ambition would make this happen; hence, in desperation, I majored in every aspect of Land Surveying. Usually you are expected to major in one aspect, but I was equally good at Land Surveying, Geodesy, Cartography, Photogrammetry, Hydrography and Engineering Surveying. I embarked on all this because I did not want to ever become unemployed or obsolete in my industry. I reasoned that should there ever be an over-subscription for related work or an unemployment crisis, I would have several other options available to me that I could fall back on.

While at George Wimpey, I developed an interest in Construction Survey and therefore majored in Highway Design and Construction. To date, none of this knowledge has been wasted. Everything learnt remains quite fresh in my brain and is being applied to Kingdom work on mission fields, an example of which is the Jesus City Project *(visit www.cftchurches.org for more details about that project)*. I continued studying and seeking knowledge because I desired to become an autonomous human being. I did not want any church to incapacitate me financially, due to the decision of some unscrupulous humans who had completely lost touch with God. I was also working towards the goal that when I became wealthy, I would help ministers set up programmes that would sustain their loved ones, should they suffer untimely death, hopefully putting an end to the predicament suffered by many wives and children of deceased ministers.

Jesus told Peter, 'when you are comforted, raise up your brothers'. I have seen many pastors in my travels across the globe who belong to so-called big churches with whopping bank accounts, yet they have no pension plan or health insurance for their pastors, neither do they remunerate them adequately. Needless to say, consideration of educating their pastor's children does not even come into play. As much as I abhor superfluous living, which some pastors engage in today, it was also a plight to behold the pastors' circumstances in my teen years. In some churches today, the situation remains the same, but in Christ Faith Tabernacle we uphold Jesus' instruction to Peter to the letter.

One of the reasons I don't believe in setting up churches in every city, village or town the Lord sends me to is because I don't believe I am the only one that will conquer the whole earth. If anyone imagines they or their church alone is capable of such, that person has stopped running with a godly vision and is thus pursuing a personal ambition. We have been to some parts of the world where people sent by God in those regions struggle financially. Instead of starting our own church, in such circumstances, we support them spiritually and financially and they don't have to bear our name; that's what church is all about.

Personal commission from Jesus Christ.

Soon after leaving George Wimpey, I became a freelance surveyor and worked until 1983 when I decided to come to England. Once in England, I commenced my studies in Land Survey and Mapping Sciences at the former North East London Polytechnic, now known as University of East London. Upon completion, I decided to proceed for a PhD in Remote Sensing and Satellite Geodesy. In order to accomplish that, I needed a scholarship, so I went to Nigeria in 1984 to seek a scholarship from the British Council.

It was during this period in Nigeria while we were seated at the dinner table, that one of those present, a prophetess, was asked to pray/bless the meal. She prayed for over 30 minutes and then began to prophesy and said: 'Alfred, Alfred, thus saith the Lord, this is your last meal for three days; after this meal you must go into the room and meet with Me for three days without seeing the sun for what I'm about to reveal to you. You must not eat or drink for the three days.'

After that meal I went to my room and locked myself up and began to fast for three days without food and water and praying every three hours. My wife was with me fasting as well but breaking at 6pm every day. She said if God was going to reveal something to me, she wanted to be part of the revelation. During this fasting, I prayed daily at 9am, 12 noon, 3pm, 6pm, 9pm, 12 midnight, 3am and 6am.

> *Suddenly, the wall of my room opened up and I looked through it upwards. ...*

At about 3.30am on the fourth day after praying, as I sat down on the chair resting, something supernatural took place.

Suddenly, the wall of my room opened up and I looked through it upwards. From the heavens I saw someone stretch out a massive carpet which rolled all the way down to my room in one swift movement. The sight of the carpet, if you could really call it that, was so regal and it enthralled me. Unexpectedly, I saw the Son of Man, the Lord Jesus Christ, walking down on the path created by the laid out carpet. I recognised who He was because I had seen Him before. His gait is like no other, what an awesome presence to behold! He majestically walked into my room and I immediately jumped to my feet in reverence to Him. In human appearance, to me, Jesus stands about 6 feet tall (as He appeared to me on this occasion) and the most amazing thing about Him is that He takes on various other forms as well.

There was one occasion when He appeared to me as a human figure wrapped in a cloud. You could see the human form but surrounding Him was endless cloud. It is certainly an experience I have never seen on earth and most certainly impossible to describe with mere words. When the cloud first unwrapped, I saw something like a half moon slowly leaping out from its horizon and then the face of the Lord appeared, covered with immeasurable and intensely illuminating light. The strong beam that emanated from Him is beyond description. I opened my mouth to try and ask Him for power but I could not utter any word. He smiled at me and then turned His face away and very swiftly disappeared amidst the clouds. At the time I had this first encounter with Jesus, I had been praying for some time for the baptism of the Holy Spirit.

> *His eyes seemed to see right through my very soul and He understood my thoughts even though I did not say anything aloud...*

However, on this occasion, when He majestically walked into my room He was dressed in an ancient Roman soldier's regalia. His eyes seemed to see right through my very soul and He understood my thoughts even though I did not say anything aloud. Contrary to popular belief, Jesus is neither a white man nor a black man; His skin is almost an amalgamation of both complexions giving Him a tanned, almost Arabian-like, skin tone. He looked at me with eyes that spoke of immeasurable love and compassion that brought such tranquillity to my soul and said,

'Go back to London and start the work.' I replied, 'But Lord I'm a land surveyor and that is what I'm doing'. Jesus simply answered, 'What you should do first you now do last.'

Jesus had in His hand a unique golden rod, a Bible, a black bishop's gown and a collar. He stretched the gown towards me and as I thought of how to receive them from Him, suddenly the gown came upon me without me reaching out to receive it. Many people have seen me wearing a black gown like a bishop's on special occasions without knowing the reason why I wear it. The gown represents a close replica of what the Lord Jesus had in His hand when He commissioned me into ministry. That's why, to this day, I still wear these gowns because it is ceremonious to me, a reminder of my commissioning. Once I had the gown on, Jesus then gave me the rod He held and the Bible. I placed both the rod and the Bible in my left hand and Jesus took my right hand and said, 'Let's go.'

I instantly saw my spirit depart from my physical body as we both began to glide through clouds into more clouds. The exhilarating sensation of this form of travel, although a spectacular experience, must have lasted about 45 minutes in reality, but it felt much less to me as I found the experience totally amazing. The best way I can describe it is like travelling in a see-through aeroplane at a much faster speed. Who needs an aeroplane when you have this, I thought? All too soon, we arrived in England. Having lived there, I knew where we were and I even knew what part of England we had arrived in – it was Westminster, just by the bridge, where a hotel has recently been erected but at the time of that encounter the place was empty.

The journey, however, turned out to be a small experience compared with the scenery that beheld me in Westminster. Once again, I experienced seeing myself outside of my body. I saw myself preaching to a sea of people. The numbers were too many to even guess; literally hundreds of thousands would be a modest guess. The sea of faces listening to me stretched all the way down to Trafalgar Square with an overflow extending to Buckingham Palace Road, and the whole of Westminster Bridge area and beyond. The whole area was covered by innumerable people crying out for the Lord Jesus. All the churches within the vicinity were overflowing with people. Many traditional church leaders were overwhelmed with the numbers of people trooping into their churches and thus began to seek help to support them in shepherding the people. Undeniably, a day will come in London when people as numerous as the sands on the seashore will gather together only for one purpose: the Lord Jesus.

Among the people I was preaching to there where blacks in tens of thousands but they were only about 1% of those present. No vehicle was able to move and no one was able to walk anywhere. It was a sight to behold.

At present, the UK appears to be a tough nation surrounded by an embodiment of a very active network of Satan masquerading within its borders. Some people look at the state of this nation and think: can God ever redeem the UK? But I assure you of this truth: the time is drawing near when every city in the UK will be restored to the Lord. This is a very minor thing for God to do, for every man's heart is in His hands. As believers, we can overcome the stronghold of Satan in this country through fasting, praying and studying the written word of the Lord.

After the Westminster experience, the Lord took me to other places and other parts of the UK in that encounter. I saw throngs of people saved and healed and uncountable miracles occurring in an explosive manner. What I saw was not a revival where one individual appeared be a superstar. It was a revival where all churches were filled with people to overflowing. The revival broke down the barriers of denominations and their various doctrines.

We finally returned to London, and we sat down and Jesus began conversing with me. I was enthralled and enjoyed the discussion so much that I was not looking at Him. At one point, I decided to look over to my left side to His face, but now His face was no longer there! All I could see were these two large and very long legs. They were so long that I had to raise my eyes to follow the length of them. My eyes followed the legs all the way up into the clouds. The amazing thing was I was now positioned between His legs, making Him appear to be standing over me. Far into the skies, His knees upwards were enshrouded in the clouds and I could no longer see the face of Him who had been speaking with me. However, as He continued speaking to me, His voice was as though we were just walking side-by-side. The conversation continued until I realised that somehow we had got back to my house in Lagos where He again left me with the words, 'Go now and start the work.'

His departure was as sudden as His arrival and abruptly the wall of my room began to close up once more while He disappeared into the clouds. I had experienced the most life-changing incident of my life during the encounter with Jesus and, at first, felt too amazed to move or do anything.

I realised that I had received a divine call into ministry that was not subject to questioning or arguments. This call was not as a result of the conviction of an individual or the consensus of a group of people, but from the Lord Jesus Himself. I came out of my room a different man. This encounter defined who I became thereafter: a fearless man who owed apology to no man for declaring the true word of God. Neither do I fear untimely death because I know that He who has called me is always around me. It is impossible for evil forces to afflict me as long as I continue to teach and walk in His truth. I will always maintain this truth because I testify about the only true God, our Saviour Jesus Christ and the Holy Spirit.

When I came out from seeking the face of the Lord, my aunt, who was present when I was instructed to fast and pray for three days, asked me what the Lord had told me when He visited me. I told her 'Nothing' because before I came out of the praying room

> *S*he placed her right foot inside the threshold of the house and refused to enter further!

the morning after my encounter, I had prayed and asked the Lord for confirmation of what He had revealed to me. I had never desired to become a pastor and the Bible says by two or three witnesses the truth will be established. I wanted confirmation and I did not want to tell anyone before I got the confirmation. I did not have to wait long for my confirmation.

While I was still being pressed for details of my encounter from my curious aunt, a prophetess called at our home. She placed her right foot inside the threshold of the house and refused to enter further! When asked why she stayed where she was, she said the Lord had instructed her not to put her two feet inside our home. My aunt became alarmed and began to plead earnestly with the prophetess. However, the prophetess remained where she was and delivered her message from the threshold.

She narrated what the Lord had told me in my encounter with Him down to the smallest detail, which left no question in my mind that God had revealed it to her, and she left immediately without turning back. My aunt began rejoicing, dancing and praising God for having lived to see the fulfilment of the prophecies that had been spoken over my life when my mother had conceived me so many years ago. She was elated and I was more astounded than ever about how God was making His plans for my life known to me.

Still radiating with the aura of Jesus' presence, I went to visit my spiritual mother, who had mentored me in my early Christian years. As I rushed to embrace her, she fell back and went into a deep trance and did not gain full consciousness until about an hour later. She reaffirmed what the Lord had revealed to me in the vision when He visited me. In fact she told me everything, word for word. However, she told me that the word 'Go now and start the work now', which the Lord had said, would not commence for another ten years. She looked at me thoughtfully and reassured me that I would not struggle financially concerning the work the Lord had sent me to accomplish.

Empowerment by God

Just as I have seen Jesus face to face, so too have I been privileged to be in the presence of God the Father. This was a unique encounter that left me awestruck. My first encounter with

God occurred without any major preceding event in contrast with my encounter with Jesus calling me into ministry. While I was asleep one evening, the Father took me to a place in heaven that I can describe as full of trees. They were of such an array that it looked like a never-ending deep forest, filled with trees that were wide and high without end. The Almighty God, with the little finger of His right hand, chopped down a tree and carved out a royal chair from that tree. I can't tell you how He did it, but He did it. He then took me to a river where he immersed me, but I could breathe and speak while under the water. He talked and played with me as He bathed me in that river, just as a mother does with her child. I saw myself take on the form of a baby in that encounter. With that same little finger, He made a crown and sewed a very beautiful robe which he dressed me in and sat me on the royal chair He had crafted. He then picked up the chair and placed it on the centre of His right palm and raised it to just about His chest area and asked me to repeat the following words after Him: 'I have lifted you high above all your enemies, their hands can never reach you any more.' After repeating those words, I looked up to see the face of the person speaking with me and as I gazed up, the middle line on His palm became like a vertical ridge and I could not see His face, so I said, 'Lord, let me see your face.' He replied, 'No one sees the face of the Father and lives.'

So I said to myself, 'Oh, I am in the presence of God the Father' and in that excitement I woke up. The Bible talks about the hand of God and I can testify to it that God does truly have a hand: I have seen it *Exodus 15: 6, Isaiah 49: 16 and Ezekiel 37: 1.*

The Cherub

After many years in the ministry, I became concerned about a particular trend. Whenever I attended a function organised by fellow ministers, most of their discussions revolved around their wealth: their latest car, home, new business, etc. However, that was not all of it. A good number of them were also behaving very badly, an absolute contradiction of their teachings and sermons. Due to my position in ministry, I am privy to a host of information about various top ministers who lead lives with double standards. I looked around me and wondered why so much was happening, with many people getting away with doing the exact opposite of what God has mandated us as His shepherds to the flock. It grieved my heart and I lost the desire to live in such a world. This got to the point that I did not think about what my wish would do to my wife and children but became consumed with the desire to leave this debased earth. I began praying fervently to God that I wanted to come home where everything was so beautiful and I meant the prayer with the whole of my heart.

Each time I preached in the church I would tell the congregation that I wanted to depart to heaven, until a sister came up to me after service one Sunday and said, 'Dad, please stop announcing that you want to die, it gets us very upset. There is still much more work for you to do and if you die who would take care of us?' It was only then it dawned on me that I might not have completed my God-given task on earth and it would be a travesty to die before completing my work. Moreover, I realised that God was speaking to me through this spiritual daughter of mine. God had sent me to this world for a purpose and how much of this work had I accomplished? Immediately, I changed my prayer from seeking to depart from this earth, to seeking to know how much work I had done on earth. I began to enquire of God of my works on earth, how much had I done and what degree remained of my whole work on earth in proportion to what had been done? I also wanted to know what was left for me to still do. While in the process of asking, on the third night, when I got home after I had finished praying, I read my Bible before nodding off to sleep with a wish in my heart: 'Lord, oh that you show me a cherub, I've never seen one and I would really love to see one.'

Immediately I closed my eyes to go to sleep, I was caught up into heaven. I saw from afar, in the northern hemisphere, the throne of the Father. As I gazed at the throne in utter delight and amazement, I saw a gate, which was marked by blinding light, beginning to slowly open up and a very small beam of light came through the gate, heading towards me. As it got nearer, it took the form of a baby with six beautiful wings and a white/silky looking skin. The nearer it got to me, it began to grow into a chubby baby, and I thought in my mind, 'What a small angel'. Then I heard the voice of the Father say, 'Do not call this angel a small angel because this angel has the power to take America off the face of the map.'

When the Cherub landed and stood in front of me, we were the same height. I was amazed in my heart and thought, 'It's a baby angel.' The Cherub looked into my eyes with confidence as though saying, 'I know what you are thinking' and smiled. He then said, 'I am a Cherub who stands in the presence of the Father. Yesterday night you were praying and you asked the Lord to send you a Cherub. I have now come as an answer to that request.'

The Cherub stretched his hands from the left to the right and a book appeared suspended in mid air right before us. On that book was my real name, written in the handwriting of God, in gold. I could not read it but I could see the letters. The book was black, with precious stones embedded in it and the angel opened the book and I saw myself from birth, everything I had done till the very moment I lay down to rest that night; the only aspect of my life that I did not see were my sins and my mistakes. Isn't it amazing that God's words are for ever true? It states in *Hebrews 8: 12*

"For I will forgive their wickedness and will remember their sins no more" and in Isaiah 43:25 "I, even I, am He who blots out your transgressions, for my own sake, and remembers your sins no more."

All that he showed me was the work I had done on earth with God's help up to the very time I had the visitation.

I said in my heart, 'Oh my God, I have only finished 25% of the work I am supposed to do on earth!' I thought that at my age, I would definitely not be able to complete the remaining work I was supposed to do on earth before I died. The angel looked into my eyes and said, 'Don't say that you cannot finish your work.' One of the unique things about heaven is that you can see each other's thoughts, nothing is hidden and people communicate by thought. The cherub then told me, 'From now on, your work will be exponential' and I thought again in my heart, 'Oh, wow, angels even understand mathematics!' He looked at me and smiled knowing my thought, and then he replied, 'You can finish your work in five, ten or fifteen years', as he used his hands to draw an exponential graph, 'I'll show you what you would do next ...'

Just then my wife opened the door and walked into our bedroom and I woke up. My primary thought at the time was that my wife had hindered me from seeing what was to be the next line of my operations on earth, but on second thoughts I came to the conclusion that it had been the Lord Himself who hindered the angel from showing me what was next, as He wanted to show me Himself. I therefore began to pray, 'Lord I want to see you.'

I prayed from October 2008 until January 2009, when the Lord appeared to me and showed me the amount of work I had left to do on earth and told me how a Christian or anyone can pray in such a manner that God is bound to answer. The Lord Jesus brought before me an elder (bishop) who had sinned and was praying superficially for forgiveness from the Lord. The Lord answered him and said, 'I will not forgive you' and began to walk away, but as he was going it dawned on me that if the Lord turns His back on a person, Satan will make a meal of the person's life. So I began to weep from the depths of my soul, begging for mercy on behalf of the elder. My heartfelt cry for mercy stopped the Lord in His stride and, as much as He tried to move His feet, my tears incapacitated him. He looked me straight in the eyes and said. 'Son, if anyone prays to me about anything the way you have just done, it is impossible for me not to answer.' It was also on that occasion that He instructed me, saying 'Now start writing books', which I could not commence until a few years later.

Not long after that encounter, every desire to die completely evaded me as doors to missions and crusades in various parts of the world opened up to me, especially in the African region where I ministered to heads of states of African nations, organisations and various other entities of prominent repute, including having a headlong collision with witches and wizards who succumbed to the glorious power of Jesus Christ. This visible victory over Satan's agents led to the salvation of some kings: about eight kings in one meeting and a few others at other times. God did many miraculous signs and wonders in those nations. *(See my book The Call of an Apostle for more details on my trips to the nations)*

" The angel patiently said, 'The time is up, you have to
go back.' ..... the angel tried to pick me up and I
resisted by twisting my leg against the leg of the
angel. We both had a scuffle and the angel could not
do anything because I was able to counter his effort
strength-wise, ...(Genesis 32: 24–32). I was therefore
able to resist the angel "

3

THE FIRST EXPERIENCE
OF HEAVEN

*A*lthough I have shared some of my experiences with you, I would like to point out that my experience during the three days of fasting was not my first encounter of heaven. What is probably most important to you while reading this book is to grasp an understanding of how to come into the place of your own first encounter of heaven.

Let me emphasize a key element you cannot do without if you want to encounter heaven, and that is desire. The yearning to encounter heaven has to be strong within you, with a tangible air of expectation every day. I was exceedingly curious to know what Jesus looks like. The desire to see Him consumed me and so I started observing the hours of prayer – by praying every day at 6am, 9am, 12 noon and 3pm. During those prayer times, my key prayer point was, 'Lord, what do you look like? I want to see you Lord, reveal yourself to me.' I repeated those words over and over again with a heart of utmost curiosity and earnest expectation. Those were not just words that were only coming from my lips, but every ounce, breath and zest within me also yearned for His presence. I was not fasting at this time. However, fasting cannot be used as a substitute for a lifestyle that is consistently engrossed in things of the Father, Son and the Holy Spirit.

What fasting does is this: it invokes the power of God and propels your body to a place where it becomes very attractive to the supernatural powers of God. When fasting, if you can also commit yourself to constant praying and reading the scriptures, within a very short space of time your mind becomes detached from earthly things, thus opening you up to angelic visitation. What my curiosity and earnest prayers did was to bring me to a

> *I* felt a tap on my leg and opened my eyes. I saw a figure of an angel. This angel looked like a man...

place of deep intimacy with God, such that I did not have any other thought throughout the day than 'Lord I want to see you.' When I was walking along the road, I expected to see the Lord; when I sat down, I expected an angel to appear to me. I became very aware of my immediate environment to the extent that whenever I heard a sound, I would assume it was the Lord coming to visit me. This is the sort of state of mind that anyone who wants to see Jesus should have, because it invokes encounters with the Lord. That led to my very first time of having a clear visibility of heaven. On the twenty-eighth day after praying at 12 midnight, I felt a tap on my leg and opened my eyes. I saw the figure of an angel. This angel looked like a man and was about 6 feet tall. I instinctively knew he was an angel because when he stretched out his hands to me, I saw my spirit leaving my physical body as it lay on my bed. We went up to the sky and landed in heaven. Angels appear in various forms; they are neither black nor white-skinned creatures. In the physical form they look like a slim Arab person with tanned skin.

I saw Father Abraham

The angel took me to a field surrounded by hedges and filled by an uncountable number of people. They were all of the same height and size, dressed in immaculate white garments, holding handkerchiefs in one hand and a palm frond in the other hand. They appeared to be talking to one another. As we got to the edge, the angel holding my hand stopped and another angel stretched out his arm to take me in. This new angel led me to a sitting area beside an altar. Seated on the altar was a man with long silvery and curly hair. His beard was also white and very long. As I got nearer to the throne, I thought it was Jesus, so I went over to him, to bow and worship him. But the angel that escorted me there stopped me and said, 'Don't worship him because he is a mortal man like you; meet Abraham, the father of faith.' I looked at him very closely and said to myself, 'Is this the Abraham we read about in the Bible?' and to my amazement the angel took me directly to Father Abraham who shook my hands and said, 'Come over to the right-hand side.' I stood beside him on the right-hand side and one angel gave me a trumpet to blow. I replied saying, 'I do not blow a trumpet on earth', then the angel repeated his first instruction, 'Take, blow.'

One thing I have observed with angels is that they don't argue with you, because they speak the words of God. Like amplifiers, they open their mouths and project what God is saying through their lips and so they don't have the privilege of changing their mind or arguing with people. I realised that there was no point in arguing and the third time the angel said 'Blow', I hurriedly put the trumpet in my mouth and blew, and I really blasted it. When I started to blow the trumpet, I began to play this song: 'For ever, oh Lord, thy word is settled in heaven, it is settled'.

Up to that time I had never heard that song, but the moment I began to sound the trumpet the angels joined in, and instantly all the musical instruments you can think of – and those not yet created here on earth – took up the tune and angels began to sing. The melody of their voices cannot be described. All the people in white began worshipping too, with their voices sounding like the rich strong waves of a mighty sea. They lifted up their palm fronds and handkerchiefs and waved them first to the right, and then to the left; their voices were so perfect and the harmony was next to none I have ever heard on earth.

There was a particular angel beside me that really astonished me, because as I blew the trumpet I had my sight on this particular angel. My bewilderment came when this angel opened his mouth and started singing; sounds from every instrument flowed freely from this angel's lips. I could hear percussion, bass guitar, lead guitar, trumpet, trombone, xylophone, keyboard, violin and every other instrument you can name. As well as the sound of these instruments coming forth from the angel, I could also hear voices that had all the musical tones such as treble, alto, tenor and bass. The angel was singing at the same time. That such euphony could emanate from one set of lips bedazzled my mind and I could barely contain my excitement.

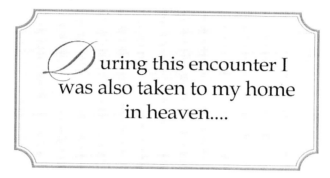

During this encounter I was also taken to my home in heaven....

You will not be surprised that the world has now invented a machine that, when you can sing into it, mimics your voice in various notes. How it works is that one man sings in their own voice and the machine sings all the parts. But I first saw this in heaven, which makes the discovery in relation to what I have seen happen in heaven so exciting. There is no depth of discovery that man can find in this realm that is truly new. This angel that was singing all instruments and voice chords at once had the figure of a very young woman; she was beautiful beyond perfection. Bear in mind that angels don't have gender but in their build they have similar looks to either the shape of a woman or of a strong young male. There are also cherubs and they look like a baby that is very robust and beautiful. Everything in heaven captivated my attention because the beauty that surrounded me was a joy to behold.

During this encounter I was also taken to my home in heaven. Outside my home was an angel singing and worshipping God with various instruments accompanying the song, all from the mouth of this one angel. We entered the house and even the words 'extremely exquisite' do not do justice to the description of my heavenly abode. Even as a surveyor familiar with construction and building work, I still do not have words to describe the pillars therein. Surprisingly, when we left my home, the angel was still sitting outside the front door singing, so I asked the Lord, 'Why is this angel outside my home singing?' And the Lord answered, 'This angel has been positioned to always sing outside your home because I know on earth you love to worship me.'

was getting desperate by this time and practically shouted at him, 'Did YOU hear me, I'm not going!'....

As I was glorying in my new and thrilling experience, the angel that had brought me to heaven appeared and said it was time for me to go back. I looked at him to see if he was joking and replied saying, 'Go where?' Since he could not argue, the angel repeated, 'You have to go now.' I asked again, 'Go where?' and the angel replied, 'You must go back to the earth.' I could not believe this angel intended to take me away from the most beautiful place I had ever seen and I said vehemently, 'I'm not going.' The angel patiently said, 'The time is up, you have to go back.' I was getting desperate by this time and practically shouted at him, 'Did YOU hear me, I'm not going!' Seeing that I was not going to budge, the angel tried to

APOSTLE ALFRED TB WILLIAMS

pick me up and I resisted by twisting my leg against the leg of the angel. We both had a scuffle and the angel could not do anything because I was able to counter his effort strength-wise, as this was the biggest struggle of my life and I put every ounce of my strength into it (remember I used to be a boxer and I had also read about how Jacob struggled with an angel, *Genesis 32: 24–32*). I was therefore able to resist the angel.

Suddenly, I saw the cloud shift, with a beam of light showing from the higher heavens. Though I was distracted by the light, I still continued struggling with the angel. The beam of light grew nearer until it struck the angel. Without any further ado, the angel picked me up as though I weighed no more than a piece of paper in his hands. With this experience, I understood how angels are empowered by God. There is nothing God cannot achieve through them (or an angel) once they are empowered. God can phase out the whole universe with one angel because the power the angel uses comes from God.

I also believe this is one of the reasons why Satan cannot really estimate angels. If an angel appears today and is only able to do so much, if that same angel faces a battle the next time the devil assumes the angel would expend the same strength again, thereby becoming a victim of his own erroneous judgement.   This is because angels operate under different mandates and are empowered with strength that is commensurate with each mandate. The angel can do as much as the God who created the whole earth will enable him to do.

As the angel picked me up I wriggled my legs crying helplessly, 'No, no' and I cried 'No, no' till I woke up. I kept shouting on my bed 'No, no'. Then I opened my eyes and I said

'Oh my!' I had been sent back to earth where I no longer longed to be, having had a taste of heaven. That day, I prayed really hard to die from morning to 6pm. I asked God to kill me. I forgot about my wife or family as I told God I just wanted to go back to singing with the angels. I wept so much but God didn't answer my prayers. About 6pm that evening, I realised it was not God's will for me to die and made up my mind to dedicate myself to earnestly seeking God's face one more time.

On the thirtieth day after my first encounter and through prayers, Jesus appeared to me again and I have had several journeys to heaven since then. I have come to understand that these encounters are given to me as a message for God's people.

4
CHRIST FAITH TABERNACLE (CFT) INTERNATIONAL CHURCHES

Connection with Olivet Deptford Baptist Church

Before I left for Nigeria in 1984, I had been attending New Testament Church of God. However, after the encounters I had during my trip to Nigeria, I was looking forward to what God would do in the UK. On arrival, my wife and I prepared to go to church, but as it is customary for us to pray before we go out, we got down on our knees and began to pray. In an open vision, the Lord spoke audibly to me and said, 'You will not go to that church today. You will go out of this street and follow the road and turn left. There you will find an overhead bridge and as you pass under the bridge just at the junction you will find a church and that's where you will worship today.' I told my wife what the Lord had just said and she asked me, 'What about the place we usually attend, will they not be expecting us there?' I told her to forget about that place since we were under a new instruction. She asked again, 'What if there is no bridge on the road?' I told her we would have to follow the instructions of God first and then see what would turn out.

As the Lord had earlier told me the name of the road, we went in search of it. When we turned left as directed by God in the vision, behold right there before us was the bridge. As we passed the bridge, we saw the church and went inside the building. The name of the church to this day is still Olivet Deptford Baptist

41

Church, pastored by Pastor Don Bishop at that time. There were only about fifteen people in attendance that Sunday. The majority of them were very old, with the exception of a couple who were young adults at the time.

It was a very cold and quiet place. I murmured silently to the Lord that I would not be able to stay there. The minister was the only person speaking and singing excitedly, while others were passive. When he said, 'Praise God', nobody answered him. As someone who came from a very vibrant church, it was really difficult to comprehend how I would fit into this new fellowship. Just then the Lord said to me, '*He that is whole needs no physician, but he that is sick.*

He pointed me out and asked me to join him on the pulpit to share my testimony. '....

If you would work for me, this is where you will begin and you will be able to count your blessings and name them one by one.' Still locked in my conversation with the Lord, I heard Pastor Don Bishop say that the Holy Spirit had just told him that this young man who was visiting had a testimony to share. He pointed me out and asked me to join him on the pulpit to share my testimony.

I realised this was God's confirmation that He had sent us to this church. I told the church how the Lord had directed my wife and I to their midst. And that was how I became a member of Olivet Deptford Baptist Church. While a member, I asked

Pastor Don for the attendance register and prayed every midnight petitioning God for all who had left the church to return. Every Sunday I would stand at the door to welcome visitors asking them their names as they entered, so I could tick them off on the register as a returned member. In no time the church membership grew from 15 to about 120.

Not long after this the Lord visited me and said, 'Every time you get to my genealogy you don't read it, you just flip over it, but I have now come to teach you' and he opened the Bible – first to the book of Matthew and then to Luke – and taught me, tracing the links to Mary and Joseph. He taught me for six hours but when I woke up I forgot all about it. Subsequently, I began to pray to the Lord to remind me of the lesson He had taught me. After several months of prayer, the Holy Spirit spoke to me saying, 'When it is time for you to teach it you will remember, for he has put it in your spirit for the right time.' I guess that's why my teaching about the genealogy of Christ is astonishing. The reason is because the Master himself unravelled the mystery concerning His birth to me.

As I was used to having night vigils in my former church back in Nigeria, I asked Pastor Don Bishop to permit me to start a night vigil at the church and he agreed. It was there that I pioneered the first all-night vigil every Friday in London from 1984. Many miracles occurred during the night vigil and people began to speak in tongues. The news soon spread to the Presbytery and the whole church began attending. After four years some members of the Presbytery rose up against the revival. They demanded that I should stop hosting the meeting. I refused. They bothered Pastor Don Bishop so much with various allegations of trying to distort the Baptist doctrines by speaking in tongues and conducting healing services. In one of our church committee meetings a leader stood up and said, "If God had called me into ministry, I should leave the church and go back to Africa and the Lord who has sent me, should bring me back to confirm that He has sent me". The man said this because he knew the church was intending to assist me in obtaining a visa extension as a clergyman.

This challenge brought me to the point of realising that it was time for God to show Himself as the one who had sent me. I declared that I would go back to Africa and let God take perfect control. During the night vigil the following Friday, I announced to the church that I would be returning to Nigeria but did not tell them why. One of the members, Mrs Adisa about whom the Lord had given me a prophecy that she would conceive and have a child, ran towards me and held my leg. She said, 'Where is the child your God promised me?' Compassion filled my heart for her and I said to her, 'By the time I return to Britain you will be three months pregnant.' It was only after uttering that prophecy that I realised I would be gone for more than three months. The situation with Mrs Adisa was that she does not menstruate and as such could not conceive a child. Most of the famous gynaecologists in the UK had seen her at one time or the other and none of them could help her. She and her husband had tried various other means to have a child but were unsuccessful until we met. Today, Mrs Adisa has three children; one of them has just graduated from university. She still does not menstruate, but the God of heaven opened her womb to bear the three children she has today. *(See The Call of an Apostle for the full testimony).*

"...As I looked further, I saw the angel that looks after that church, seated above the church. There was a deep and tangible darkness that could be physically touched over the church..."

5

CHRIST FAITH TABERNACLE NIGERIA

*F*ollowing my departure from Olivet Deptford Baptist Church, I returned to Nigeria in 1989 to seek a scholarship to study for a PhD in Satellite Geodesy and Remote Sensing. My wife continued working as a senior flight stewardess with the former Nigeria Airways. On one of her trips, she met Prophet Obadare of Nigeria who is also my spiritual father. This prophet is registered blind but was still able to spot my wife from among the other cabin crew members on board that flight. He called for her and asked after her husband and also said, 'Your husband is a pastor.' She replied saying that her husband was one of his sons and used to work with some of his pastors as an intercessor whenever they were to organise a crusade.

Prophet Obadare asked her to tell her husband to come and see him as the Lord had need of him in his ministry. When my wife told me this, I initially did not want to go to see him because I had recently experienced disappointment in serving within a ministry, but as I told my wife, I heard the audible voice of God say, 'Go to him.' So I went to visit him. He was at a meeting at the time but when he heard I was the one, he left the meeting to attend to me. He asked me to come over and sit by his side in his car, while we drove to his house. This was a huge privilege because when I had served under him, I was almost at the sixteenth level of subservience to him. He reiterated that the Lord told him I should pastor one of his churches in London. I looked at him and told him that the Lord had not spoken to me concerning that. He looked amazed and perplexed because at that time it was considered a privilege by many to be associated with his ministry. I told him that the teachings we received from him, which were passed on by Apostle Joseph Ayo Babalola, taught us that until the Lord confirms a word to us we must not make any move, especially when it comes to spiritual matters and mandates. I asked him to excuse me for five minutes to ask the Lord in prayer.

Prophet Obadare agreed. As I began to pray, the Lord told me all that had transpired in an arm of his ministry, the people involved, the root cause and solution, and what would happen in six months and a year later in that parish. The Lord then told me that my own personal ministerial work would not start until about three years and half years later and that in the interim I could work with anyone and concluded that my gift would be beneficial to the Prophet's church. I came out of the prayer room and explained this to him. He confirmed the revelation as being correct and accurate. That's how I was ordained as a CAC pastor. I was given a letter to the supreme council of CAC who then absorbed me into the CAC church and was subsequently posted to CAC, 28, Olowu Street, Lagos, Nigeria - where I was born and nutured as a Christian from a very tender age.

Following my induction into the CAC Olowu branch, as a clergy, I was appointed to minister the following Sunday. At this I called for some of the members of the Light of the World, who were my colleague intercessors from 1967, to start interceeding for my preaching assignment the following Sunday. This is due to the revelation I saw in 1987 about the church and I believed it was time to deliver the message.

1989 Revival (CAC Olowu, Lagos)

In 1987 an angel appeared to me, and took me to the mid heavens. Above me was the throne room of the Father and beneath was CAC Olowu, Lagos Nigeria. I was made to look down at the Church. As I looked further, I saw the angel assigned to the church sitting above the church. There was a deep and tangible darkness that could be physically touched within the church.

As I moved closer I heard the angel singing the last verse of this song:

Thy kingdom come, O God,
Thy rule, O Christ, begin;
Break with Thine iron rod
The tyrannies of sin.

Where is Thy reign of peace,
And purity, and love?
When shall all hatred cease,
As in the realms above?

When comes the promised time
That war shall be no more
Oppression, lust and crime
Shall flee Thy face before?

We pray Thee, Lord arise,
And come in Thy great might;

Revive our longing eyes,
Which languish for Thy sight.

Men scorn Thy sacred name
And wolves devour Thy fold;
By many deeds of shame
We learn that love grows cold.

O'er heathen lands afar
Thick darkness broodeth yet;
Arise, O morning Star,
Arise, and never set.

('Thy Kingdom Come O God' was written by LEWIS HENSLEY in 1867.)

47

From the high heavens I heard the voice of the Father saying three times, *'Revelation 2: 4'*, and then He said, 'Go and tell them now!' That scriptural verse reads thus: *"Yet I hold this against you: You have forsaken your first love."*.

The angel brought me down to the entrance of the church and we entered. I saw a man who was responsible for the darkness I had earlier seen in the church. About two months afterwards, Professor Imevbore, a senior minister of CAC, visited me and I recounted my vision about the church to him. He enlightened me about the predicaments in the church and I asked whether he could deliver my message and he told me that at the right time, the Lord would make a way for me to address the issue myself, since I was the one sent.

This is the reason why I believe that ministering that Sunday, would serve as an opportunity to deliver the message; hence my invitation of the intercessors to join me. What a wonderful day that turned out to be! I preached for three hours and no one moved. God did a lot of miracles. The presbytery was very impressed and declared a crusade which lasted 90 days. A revival broke out in the crusade that shook the whole of CAC in 1989. We had over 1,200 people saved and some were delivered from witchcraft and baptized with the Holy Spirit.

It was at this crusade that a gentleman vomited a live lizard which often made him convulse, exhibiting the signs of an epileptic. God moved in a mighty way. The dead were raised, the crippled walked, the blind saw, people were brought from their hospital beds to be healed, and they were healed and perfectly restored. It was a very powerful crusade.

During this crusade there was an atheist doctor who brought one of his patient, saying if God healed the patient, then he would believe. This patient was brought on a stretcher and had been bed ridden for 8 years, after all medical effort had failed. During the message I commanded him to rise up on his feet and then the power of God came upon him, shook him and instantly he got up and started running, completely healed. At this the Atheist doctor came forward to surrender his life to Christ.

Another outstanding day was when by word of Knowledge, the Lord said he would heal a cripple child at the meeting, haven announced this, two women raised their hands and the Lord said the one with a girl , at this one of the hands went down while the girl was brought right to the front of the altar, with both legs crippled by polio. Suddenly as I was preaching, the power of God came upon me, I turned towards the girl and commanded her to rise up and walk. The power of God shook the girl and pulled her up from her feet and she started running. The entire church englulfed in a flame of praise as people were running to the pulpit and giving their lives to Christ.

At the end of the service I felt very sad that God had not healed the boy. In my dismay, I heard God's audible voice, He said, "tell the one with boy to bring him tomorrow". The news of this spread round the whole region.

The following day, from 2pm the hall was jammed to the outside with people. The front two rows were filled with muslim clerics, who having heard about the healing the previous day, expressed their unbelief and hence came to witness the boy's case.

While I was ministering, the power of God came upon me as it was the previous day, as I turned to the boy and said rise up in the name of Jesus! All the muslim clerics rose up from the seat to gain advantage of the sight. The boy shook under the power of God, pulled up to his feet , his legs instantly grew and expanded and he started running. The whole hall again was englufed with praises on to God, while all the muslim clerics fell face to the ground, shouting the Lord is God. They threw all their rosaries, amulets and talisman on the altarand surrendered their lives to Christ.

Several witches and witch doctors also gave their lives to Christ, some of them after ferroucious confrontations.

I can say that crusade was what God used to birth the ministry of signs and wonders in my apostolic commission.

CHRIST FAITH TABERNACLE CHURCH, LONDON

he story of how the London church began is quite unusual and very interesting. While pastoring Prophet Obadare's church in Archway, London, God once again did mighty miracles but I got accused of arresting and exposing people with demonic spirits. This led to a lot of debate about the CAC doctrines and I was told to stop or I could no longer lead the group. In light of other conflicts going on at the time within CAC, in the end, I decided to leave and began to ask the Lord about what next I should do in the UK: and the Lord told me to begin a seven-day prayer vigil. On the seventh day, the Lord gave me the name, 'Christ Faith Tabernacle', in a revelation. The Lord told me that He was sending me 'on a cradle of CAC' to build a church that would be exactly like what Apostle Joseph Ayo Babalola had built in his days, which was structured after the pattern of the book of Acts. This is also because CAC started in 1918 as Faith Tabernacle before the final change of name to Christ Apostolic Church in 1943.

I had gone to do some food shopping in the local Deptford street market where I met an old member from my night vigil sessions at the Olivet Deptford Baptist Church. This was a couple of years after I had resigned from the Church. He asked if I would consider teaching himself and some of his friends the scriptures. I accepted and invited them to my home the following week. Thirty-three people gathered at that first meeting and within a short space of time the numbers grew sporadically to the extent that we had to rent a hall, Hughes Fields Community Centre, Deptford as my home had become too small to occupy everyone. We moved locations a lot in the early years as a result of growth and several other issues associated with a new Movement. Not too long thereafter, during one of our meetings, the Lord spoke to me about a church building in New Cross Road, giving a detailed description of the building and the instruction that, 'This is the church where I want you to worship next Sunday at 2pm.' I recounted my vision to our members during our Wednesday service and asked them to meet God there on Sunday at 2pm that same week.

The next day, being Thursday, I went in search of the location, found it and contacted the pastor in charge (Father Owen) who invited me to his official residence. I recounted my vision to him and he said, 'We have never given our building to anybody and we need a committee to meet but you can tell your people that next Sunday you will meet here.' That was how Christ Faith Tabernacle church, London branch emerged on 4 March 1990. My first sermon that glorious Sunday was entitled 'I will build my church and the gate of hell shall not prevail' *(Matthew 16: 18).* This teaching was given to me in a vision by the Lord Jesus and has since become one of the driving forces behind my global operation.

Our first choirmaster, Mr Andrew Panagos, a Greek citizen by birth but an Australian by nationality, was revealed to me in a vision a week before he visited our church. In that vision I saw him playing the guitar and leading worship in our church. I saw also his wife, a keyboardist, playing the keyboard in our church. Mind you, at the time Brother Andrew was a bachelor. As I often stand by the church entrance welcoming people into the church, so when I saw Mr Panagos turn up at the church doorstep, I immediately recognised him as the brother I had seen leading worship in our church the week before. Full of excitement, I quickly rushed to fetch my guitar and handed it over to him. I then took him to the front of our choir, introduced him to them as their new worship leader and asked him to lead us in worship that morning. He looked flabbergasted and confused and asked how I knew he plays the guitar, to which I replied, 'The Lord told me.' I also gave him revelations about his wife. Not long thereafter he travelled to the USA and came back with the picture of a lady he said would soon be his wife. When I looked at the photograph, I told him that was not the woman I had seen in the vision as his wife. He soon broke up with the lady and a couple of months later brought a photograph of another lady to me. When I looked at it, this time around, I could tell it was the woman I had seen in the vision and told him she was a keyboardist. He confirmed that she was. They are both still married and serving the Lord Jesus. Mr Panagos's mother also joined our church and was instrumental in our first mission trip to Greece.

The key to what CFT stands for

The testimony at the headquarters church in London is that a lot of believers get baptised with the Holy Spirit during the Holy Ghost Convention. A good number also receive the gifts of the Spirit during the Holy Ghost Convention. The hearts of many are revisited by God through the obedience of holding this seminar which is instrumental to the success and growth that is being enjoyed by CFT church globally but particularly at the headquarters. As the Lord has instructed me, I instruct ministers reading this book to please set days aside to teach Christians about Jesus Christ and the Holy Spirit.

Another area the Lord has instructed me to uphold is the Family Clinic, where the main focus is on marriage: seeking a life partner, courtship, preparing for children and enjoying marital life.

The knowledge of Jesus Christ is what enables a man or woman to know the standard of holiness. If you are able to know the life of Christ, the way He behaves, speaks and reasons, being able to decode the mind of Christ completely, then you will easily be able to walk before God and be complete. If a believer (young or old) is not taught very well about the pre-existence of Christ, the Christ revealed in the Old Testament, the birth, the life, the ministry, the death, the resurrection of Christ and His coming again, that believer will be handicapped in the area of holiness. So also with the Holy Spirit: if the believer does not have the true knowledge of who the Holy Spirit was, who He is and who He is to come or to be for eternity, he will not have an understanding of why the Holy Spirit is on earth now, what are the works of the Holy Spirit, what the functions of the Holy Spirit are, what the gifts of the Holy Spirit are and how to earn those gifts. Such a believer cannot live life to their full potential. So the Lord told me that every branch of CFT should have a period in the church calendar for a Jesus seminar, where the focus is Christ and Christ only, as well as a time set aside for Holy Ghost convention where the main focus will be the Holy Ghost. These three special seminars: Holy Ghost Convention, Family Clinic, and Jesus Seminar are key to the meaning of what CFT stands for.

7
FREEDOM FROM DEMONIC ABODE

There have been several occasions when I have been taken to heaven by an out-of-body experience. On each of those occasions, I would see myself lying flat on the bed while my spirit floats out of it to be taken to heaven. There are numerous other men and women of God who have also shared the testimonies of their heavenly encounters as mentioned in the later chapters of this book.

A woman once visited our London church who had several unexplainable issues surrounding her life. I prayed with her consistently for quite some time with little or no change to her circumstances. One particular night, the Lord took me to a place – a pit. This pit happened to be the residing place of demons. I realised it was their abode when I saw the numerous demons living there. Just as we humans reside in our homes when we are not out and about our various duties, the demons also have their own abode. It looked like a small village and all the houses there were built to look like a hut. Behind each hut were extremely skinny-looking human beings, bent over and tied to sticks with a rope. While I was observing the goings-on at the pit, an angel appeared by my side and took me to a place where a woman was tied down. Then the angel said, 'This woman needs to be set loose, go and untie her.' As I untied the woman, I had a vexation within me and wanted to fight the demons that had bound her, but the angel spoke and said, 'We have no time for that, we must go now, our time is up.'

The angel swiftly pulled my right hand and held it firmly while I held the woman with my left hand. As we were flying into the clouds, the demons started firing sets of arrows filled with what looked like peppercorns at my body. Surprisingly, as the arrows hit me and I shook my body, all the peppercorns disappeared. I looked at the woman to see if she was okay and then realised that it was the woman who had recently visited our church and had unexplainable issues in her life. It suffices to say that once she was set free in the pit, the freedom was manifested in real life and she became free of the demonic oppression that had held her bound.

Health matters

Some time in June 2007, the Lord took me on a journey to another place to reveal something to me. It was a place where there were lots of children with physical infirmities. The Lord then instructed me to pray for these children and as I prayed an evil spirit came out of one of the children. Not long after that, at one of my crusades, a young boy was brought to me with a very strong physical disability. He was not born that way. He had been sweeping the floor at home one day, when a strong wind blew into the house and nearly knocked him out. Shortly after that he started grinding his teeth and all the terrible symptoms of this sickness began. As they brought him towards me at the crusade, I felt a lot of compassion for him and I prayed for him. Instantly he stopped grinding his teeth and he was completely healed.

What is your first reaction when you, your child or loved one falls ill? Do you address the sickness in prayer or do you simply panic? *See Matthew 17:14-17:*

14 When they came to the crowd, a man approached Jesus and knelt before him. 15 "Lord, have mercy on my son," he said.

"He has seizures and is suffering greatly. He often falls into the fire or into the water. 16 I brought him to your disciples, but they could not heal him."

17 "You unbelieving and perverse generation," Jesus replied, "how long shall I stay with you? How long shall I put up with you? Bring the boy here to me." 18 Jesus rebuked the demon, and it came out of the boy, and he was healed at that moment.

My personal observation is that in some cases of physical disabilities, there are demons responsible for some of those symptoms and I know that this is debatable, especially as some young innocent children are sometimes affected. But we cannot overlook the simple truth that demons can be responsible for certain infirmities. I sincerely empathise with the families that have had to watch their children suffer physical infirmities and pray that the power of God will touch such homes in Jesus name.

Interceding for others

It is our responsibility as children of God to always intercede for others. I had a unique experience that demonstrates the importance of intercession.

One night the Lord woke me up at around 3am to pray for a person called Brother Brian. I did not know what or understand why I was required to pray, so I started praying in the spirit (in tongues). *1 Corinthians 14:14* (NIV) says:

"For if I pray in a tongue, my spirit prays, but my mind is unfruitful."

Initially I was praying very lightly but the prayer soon became very intense such that I received a revelation as to why I should pray for Brother Brian. I saw that he was being choked in his neck and through these prayers Brother Brian was delivered from his choking state. The following day, he shared a testimony with the church about a strange occurrence that had taken place during the previous night. He narrated how he felt a strange hand around his throat almost choking him to death. He said he struggled with that hand for some minutes until, all of a sudden, its grip disappeared. How awesome is God who watches over us. If you avail yourself, God will use you to bless more lives than you can count.

There may be someone reading this who does not know how to pray. Prayer in the simplest term means communication, i.e. communication between God and man. The way that you address someone you love and respect is the same way that you may begin to address God. However, when you grasp the knowledge of His majesty and splendour, you subconsciously begin to reverence God in a much higher dimension than you would do any other person alive.

How to approach prayer and positions of prayer

I believe very much that prayer should be conducted after the pattern of Christ. There are different kinds of prayer as revealed in *1 Timothy 2: 1–2*:

"1 I urge, then, first of all, that requests, prayers, intercession and thanksgiving be made for everyone — 2 for kings and all those in authority, that we may live peaceful and quiet lives in all godliness and holiness."

In this passage Paul spoke about requests, prayers, intercessions and thanksgiving which are all arms of prayer. It is biblical to be on our knees when we are making a request to God. Jesus Christ always made requests to God on His knees. The same rule should apply when we are saying a prayer of repentance. With intercessory prayer, one can either stand or kneel, but with warfare, i.e. wrestling with the spirit over the life of someone, it's best to do this while standing.

For a prayer of thanksgiving, one can lift up holy hands to thank God while standing but it is always good to kneel down, especially when one is at home.

At other times, we may prostrate ourselves on the floor before God while praying to Him. This is also an act of worship. *2 Chronicles 20:18* states:

> "Jehoshaphat bowed down with his face to the ground, and all the people of Judah and Jerusalem fell down in worship before the LORD."

And in *John 14:13–14*, He says:

> "13 And I will do whatever you ask in my name, so that the Son may bring glory to the Father. 14 You may ask me for anything in my name, and I will do it."

So, I believe very much that prayer is the lifeline of believers. *Hebrews 5: 7* explains to us that during the days of Jesus' life on earth He offered prayers and petitions with loud cries and tears to the One who could save Him from death and He was heard because of His reverent submission. For a man to really expect God to answer his prayer, he must first submit his heart unto God. You must make sure that your heart is free from everything that can hinder you like malice, quarrels, bad thoughts, etc. It is better for you to just ignore those things that you cannot solve; such things that may make you feel frustrated. If you cannot solve a problem, why do you think about it?

If you are always thinking about problems that you cannot solve, your mind can never be clear enough to pray, so I believe very much that submission of oneself to God is as paramount as our prayer attitude to God. It must be filled with passion. You cannot pray without your emotion and expect that prayer to touch God. In this case, Jesus' emotion was revealed because He was on His knees crying aloud and shouting. Therefore sometimes we may need to pray aloud and cry out before God. Although there are other times too, when only a silent prayer would suffice; in most cases, this depends on the environment.

Prayer should be the lifeline of all Christians. There is another scripture in the book of *1 Peter 4: 7* which says that:

"The end of all things is near. Therefore be clear minded and self-controlled so that you can pray."

Show me a holy man and I will show you a man of prayer. If there is anybody who is able to control his body and is able to live a holy life, it must be somebody who is given to prayer persistently. Prayer is a very powerful tool that God has given to us, not only to communicate with Him or tell Him about the problems we have that need His attention but also to build up our own body in the area of holiness that will help us to be in tune with heaven all the time.

I also want to state here that prayer can be a means to drawing power from God. When you go before God and pray from your heart, something from God jumps on you and that is how you can acquire tremendous power from the Lord God that we serve.

The things that mark an apostle-signs, wonders and miracles-were done among you with great perseverance...
2 Cor.12:12(NIV)

WHAT IS SUCCESS?

*T*here was a time when the Lord appeared to me and asked me, 'What do you think success is?' I told him what people often say it is – financial wealth, academic knowledge, etc. – but the Lord told me that those things were not true success.

So then what is success?

Success is when a man discovers God's mandate and purpose in his life and fulfils it. The degree of fulfilment of this earthly mandate as written by God determines the degree of one's success. In fulfilling this mandate, one may not necessarily be financially rich. The mission or mandate God has sent some people does not require excessive money to be carried out and God will not permit them to be very wealthy. In other cases, He may bring vast riches as large sums of money are required to fulfil what God has sent them to do; therefore God will make this provision available. The truth is that success is determined by the extent to which we are able to fulfil our mandate with the wisdom God has given and made available to us.

Proverbs 8: 12 says: "I, wisdom, dwell together with prudence; I possess knowledge and discretion."

Prophecies

The Lord visited me and began to speak to me about the things that would happen from the year 2000 to the year 2015.

Satan is threatened because he has an understanding that the time has come for the sons of God to begin to manifest themselves. He has the understanding that there has been an onslaught on earth, beginning from the year 2000, which has brought about the deliverance and salvation of so many souls that he has held in his claws, and because of that he is triggering panic in the kingdom of man. Since man does not have the Holy Spirit, I'm talking about the kingdom of man, not the kingdom of God among men; their spirit picks up this panic, which culminates in fear – fear of the unknown. Notwithstanding, there will soon be a great move within the church of God. Many more people will get delivered from the cluster of hell because of what they will soon begin to see and hear about occurrences in the church. God will bestow power on some Christians to an extent that they will preach the word of God with great insight, power and authority. Whenever they open their mouth to preach the word of God either briefly or at length, the word they preach will carry power and authority. They will have the ability to unravel mystery from the same words and verses that have been read again and again without insight for years. The Lord revealed to me that as the power of God begins to multiply among churches, giving birth to a church that walks in purity and holiness, this move will be replicated over the nations. Very soon, the church of God will begin to have a craving that has never been experienced before in Christendom.

In the past you may have craved for the power of God, craved for the truth excitedly, only to find yourself burning low within a short space of time. However, angels of God are now on earth as co-partners. These angels are different from the guidance spirit or the ministering spirit; they are special angels that God has prepared. These angels were prepared for this end time, as God enabled them to empower His people and invoke hunger in their heart, and direct them so that they will be able to prepare the Lord's people (including you) for His glorious coming.

Anyone can be used by God if they surrender themselves to the Holy Spirit. But to see the fulfilment of God's promises over the church, the church needs to arise. If the church does not wake up from its slumber, then the church will come to a place where it calls a meeting, but people will be afraid to turn up. For that incident not to occur in our decade, the church needs to pray. The Bible *(James 5: 16b)* says, *"The effective, fervent prayer of a righteous man avails much" (NKJV) and "The prayer of a righteous man is powerful and effective" (NIV).*

When the Lord brought me to the year 2015 in that encounter, I tried to see what would happen thereafter but my vision became blurred. So I asked the Lord what would happen thereafter and the Lord turned His back to me and began to walk away and say this *(Revelation 22: 12 (NIV))*:

"Behold, I am coming soon! My reward is with me, and I will give to everyone according to what he has done" [or according to the works of their hands - my emphasis].
He continued with verses 13 and 14:

"13 I am the Alpha, and the Omega, the First and the Last, the Beginning and the End." "14 Blessed are those who wash their

robes, that they may have the right to the tree of life and may go through the gates into the city."

I believe with the whole of my heart, not by any theological conviction or by the influence of any man but from the direct influence of the maker of heaven and earth, that we are living in a time the Bible calls "perilous times" or "the end times".

Read chapter 24 of the book of *Matthew* about the signs of the end of the age. Jesus will come again and it is not a fiction. Someone may read this and think, 'What is he talking about?' What I am expressing is this: there is a God in heaven, He created the heavens and the earth and He created you, who are reading this book. Now, you might not have encountered Him but I have; I am not telling you what I read from books, or what I was taught, but I am telling you about what I have experienced.

Someone else may retort, 'What if your encounter was not real?' My response is this: if it was not real, why is it that the prophecies that the encounter has given have come to pass? Why do we command in the name of that God and cripples walk?

ANGELS

here have been times in my meetings where some people have seen angels administering divine healing to those suffering from a variety of sicknesses and diseases. Someone may ask, 'Why do you need these encounters in your life as a believer?'

The importance of heavenly encounters and coming into contact with angels during the course of your life as a victorious Christian cannot be overemphasised.

What is an angel?

You will have noticed that, apart from the cherub I mentioned in the earlier chapter, every other angel I have described in my encounters appeared as close to a human semblance as possible, e.g. none of them had wings. When you encounter an angel, there will be absolutely no doubt in your mind that you have seen an angel. (Read the story of Cornelius in *Acts 10*)

If you doubt that you have seen an angel, then what you have seen may be as a result of your imagination or a product of your own desire to see an angel. The word 'angel' means 'messenger', and is derived from the Greek word 'angelos'. If you make a careful study of your Bible, you will realise that angels are mentioned in 34 out of the 66 books. This spans both the Old Testament and the New Testament.

There are 104 appearances of angels to either men or women. The most visited person was John in the book of Revelation, who received up to 52 angelic visitations. Despite the fact that there are various mentions of angels in the Bible, you will realise that only four of them have been named. These are Gabriel, Michael, Abaddon or Apollyan, and Lucifer. Apart from Gabriel and Michael, the other three are fallen angels, that is demons.

Gabriel

Gabriel is an archangel whose name is made up of two Hebrew words: 'geber' meaning 'warrior' and 'El', meaning 'God'. Therefore, his name means 'warrior of God' or 'courageous man of God'. The archangels are used by God to carry out special assignments. *Daniel 8: 15–16* (NIV) says:

> "15 While I, Daniel, was watching the vision and trying to understand it, there before me stood one who looked like a man. 16 And I heard a man's voice from the Ulai calling, 'Gabriel, tell this man the meaning of the vision.' "

Michael

(Jude 1: 9) 9 But even the archangel Michael, when he was disputing with the devil about the body of Moses, did not himself dare to condemn him for slander but said, "The Lord rebuke you!" Also, see *Daniel 10: 13.*

Michael is an archangel like Gabriel, but is also named as one of the chief princes. Michael takes on the stance of a military leader, leading God's angelic host against satanic forces. The name Michael is a combination of Hebrew words meaning 'who is like God?'

Lucifer

Isaiah 14: 12 (NIV) says:

"12 How you have fallen from heaven, O morning star, son of the dawn! You have been cast down to the earth, you who once laid low the nations!"

Did you know that Lucifer was a cherub? Cherubim are the order of angelic beings that are continually worshipping God. Only the cherubim are given the task of protecting the glory and holiness of God and proclaiming His grace. Before he rebelled, Lucifer had the most exalted and powerful position of trust, to direct the worship of God. This is why the betrayal was of great magnitude when Lucifer decided he wanted to direct the glory meant for God to himself.

Abaddon

Revelation 9: 11 (NIV) says:

"11 They had as king over them the angel of the Abyss, whose name in Hebrew is Abaddon, and in Greek, Apollyon [that is, Destroyer]."

Abaddon, who is referred to by the Bible as 'the angel of the bottomless pit' means 'destroying angel' and his Greek name is 'Apollyon' meaning 'destroyer'.

ATTRIBUTES OF ANGELS

Angels take orders and give protection

Psalm 91: 11–13 (NIV) says:

"11 For he will command his angels concerning you to guard you in all your ways;

12 they will lift you up in their hands, so that you will not strike your foot against a stone.

13 You will tread upon the lion and the cobra; you will trample the great lion and the serpent."

Angels eat

Genesis 19: 1–3 (NIV) says:

"The two angels arrived at Sodom in the evening, and Lot was sitting in the gateway of the city. When he saw them, he got up to meet them and bowed down with his face to the ground. 2 'My lords,' he said, 'please turn aside to your servant's house. You can wash your feet and spend the night and then go on your way early in the morning.'

'No,' they answered, 'we will spend the night in the square.' 3 But he insisted so strongly that they did go with him and entered his house. He prepared a meal for them, baking bread without yeast, and they ate."

Angels direct ministers of the gospel

Acts 8: 26–31 (NIV) says:

"26 Now an angel of the Lord said to Philip, 'Go south to the road – the desert road – that goes down from Jerusalem to Gaza.' 27 So he started out, and on his way he met an Ethiopian eunuch, an important official in charge of all the treasury of the Kandake (which means 'queen of the Ethiopians'). This man had gone to Jerusalem to worship, 28 and on his way home was sitting in his chariot reading the book of Isaiah the prophet. 29 The Spirit told Philip, 'Go to that chariot and stay near it.'

30 Then Philip ran up to the chariot and heard the man reading Isaiah the prophet. 'Do you understand what you are reading?' Philip asked.

31 'How can I,' he said, 'unless someone explains it to me?' So he invited Philip to come up and sit with him."

Angels appear in dreams

Matthew 1: 20 (NIV) says:

"20 But after he had considered this, an angel of the Lord appeared to him in a dream and said, 'Joseph son of David, do not be afraid to take Mary home as your wife, because what is conceived in her is from the Holy Spirit.' "

Angels bring answers to prayers

Daniel 9: 21–23 says:

" 21 while I was still in prayer, Gabriel, the man I had seen in the earlier vision, came to me in swift flight about the time of the evening sacrifice. 22 He instructed me and said to me, 'Daniel, I have now come to give you insight and understanding. 23 As soon as you began to pray, a word went out, which I have come *to tell you, for you are highly esteemed. Therefore, consider the word and understand the vision"*

Angels have the ability to speak in tongues

1 Corinthians: 13: 1 (NIV) says:

"1 If I speak in the tongues of men and of angels, but have not love, I am only a resounding gong or a clanging cymbal."

Angels strengthen us during trials

Luke 22: 43 (NIV) says:

"43 An angel from heaven appeared to him and strengthened him."

Angels minister to the saints

Daniel 6: 22 (NIV) says:

"22 My God sent his angel, and he shut the mouths of the lions. They have not hurt me, because I was found innocent in his sight. Nor have I ever done any wrong before you, Your Majesty."

Angels guard gates

Revelation 21: 12 (NIV) says:

"It had a great, high wall with twelve gates, and with twelve angels at the gates..."

Angels need no rest

Revelation 4: 8 (NIV) says:

"8 Each of the four living creatures had six wings and was covered with eyes all around, even under its wings. Day and night they never stop saying: 'Holy, holy, holy is the Lord God Almighty, who was, and is, and is to come.' "

Angels can appear visibly

"2 Do not forget to show hospitality to strangers, for by so doing some people have shown hospitality to angels without knowing it." Hebrews 13: 2 (NIV)

Angels travel at inconceivable speeds

Revelation 8: 13 (NKJ) says:

"13 And I looked, and I heard an angel flying through the midst of heaven, saying with a loud voice, 'Woe, woe, woe to the inhabitants of the earth, because of the remaining blasts of the trumpet of the three angels who are about to sound!' "

Angels wear clothes

John 20:12 (NIV) says:

"12 and saw two angels in white, seated where Jesus' body had been, one at the head and the other at the foot."

Angels execute judgements

Matthew 13: 41–42 (NIV) says:

"41 The Son of Man will send out his angels, and they will weed out of his kingdom everything that causes sin and all who do evil. 42 They will throw them into the blazing furnace, where there will be weeping and gnashing of teeth."

Angels minister to saints of God

Matthew 4: 11 says:

"11 Then the devil left him, and angels came and attended him."

Always remember that the one God to whom we pray is the one who answers our prayers. He cares for us and meets our needs; however, He can send our answers through an angel.

10

HOW I DEVELOPED MYSELF TO EXPERIENCE THESE ENCOUNTERS

*Y*ou may be wondering how a man can build up his relationship with God to such an extent that he experiences regular trips to heaven as well as encountering the ministration of angels. Coming to this place of relationship with God and His ministering angels is not as far-fetched as it may seem.

Your personal development as a believer

Christians who have accepted Jesus as their Lord and Saviour can know the Holy Spirit and they can see the Holy Spirit. *John 16: 5–7* (NIV) says:

> *"5 Now I am going to Him who sent me, yet none of you asks me, 'Where are you going?' 6 Because I have said these things, you are filled with grief. 7 But I tell you the truth: It is for your own good that I am going away. Unless I go away, the Counsellor will not come to you; but if I go, I will send him to you."*

In *John 14*, Jesus began to speak about the Holy Spirit and verses 15–17 (NIV) say:

> *"15 If you love me, you will obey what I command. 16 And I will ask the Father, and He will give you another Counsellor to be with*

you for ever – 17 the Spirit of truth. The world cannot accept Him, because it neither sees Him nor knows Him. But you know Him, for He lives in you and will be in you."

A good number of Christians on earth stop at the first phase when they begin to speak in tongues, while some others don't even speak in tongues nor have the desire or curiosity to attempt it. There are some conscientious Christians who not only know the Holy Spirit but have decided to see the Holy Spirit because it is possible to see the Holy Spirit. The Holy Spirit came in a physical form as a dove when Jesus Christ was baptised.

Acts 2: 1–4 (NIV) says:

"1When the day of Pentecost came, they were all together in one place. 2 Suddenly a sound like the blowing of a violent wind came from heaven and filled the whole house where they were sitting. 3 They saw what seemed to be tongues of fire that separated and came to rest on each of them. 4 All of them were filled with the Holy Spirit and began to speak in other tongues as the Spirit enabled them."

We can understand from these words that the Holy Spirit came in a physical form that looked like tongues of fire. This is the generation of church era that we are in. I want you to know that you can know the Holy Spirit and you can see the Holy Spirit. While reading this you may be reflecting in your heart about the condition that is necessary to know and see the Holy Spirit. This is very simple, as Jesus said, 'if you love me you will obey my command'. However, a lot of Christians have problems with this simple instruction from Jesus, about obeying His command.

Many want to obey what they feel and think without giving any thought to what the Bible states - they depend on their own intelligence. What intelligence can they profess to have among a billion other individuals on earth, who also think and feel they know it all? If the ratio of others on earth is compared to oneself, you will discover that one's ability and knowledge is most insignificant.

Let's now compare this intelligence to the one who created the universe and all the beings therein and the billions of beings that have existed since creation. You will discover that if anyone claims to be wise in this age, they ought to dump what they profess to know and believe and should begin to fastidiously seek after what the all-knowing God of the universe knows and believes. This is when a man begins to discover the will of God (not in the areas of personal destiny) in relation to God's plan for creation.

To illustrate this further, let us take an example of an engineer who creates a machine for public use. He will write a user manual containing guidelines for accurate usage, which anyone who wishes to operate the machine can refer to. In the same manner, God is the architect of this universe: He is the one who created the heavens and earth. He has instituted principles by which this world should run, from the greatest to the minutest elements of it. Anyone who desires to operate successfully within the sphere of His creation must understand His principles. They will have to seek God's manual, which is the Holy Bible. The Bible is the only manual that God has written concerning the operations of this universe.

More importantly, to be able to fulfil what God has freely

given on earth you must conform to the ethics of the manual and that is why Jesus said that if we love Him we will obey what He commands. We show our love of God not just by coming to church but in a hearty desire to obey God. This means that you will have to crucify your emotions and your own self. Anything you do, imagine, think or decide must be weighed against the word of God as written in the Bible.

The Bible says in *Proverbs 14: 12* (NIV): "There is a way that seems right to a man, but in the end it leads to death", meaning that the end of it is destruction. Unfortunately, many of us who profess to have Christ in us, who have accepted Jesus Christ, are still bent on our own wicked ways that come out of our own self-development. These wicked ways are a snare to man. However, the Bible says that you can see Him and you can know Him, and the Bible is absolutely and incontrovertibly true.

Jesus went on to say in *John 14: 18–21* (NIV):

"18 I will not leave you as orphans; I will come to you. 19 Before long, the world will not see me any more, but you will see me. Because I live, you also will live. 20 On that day you will realise that I am in my Father, and you are in me, and I am in you. 21 Whoever has my commands and obeys them, he is the one who loves me…"

What I did, which every believer can do; was to diligently seek the face of God and to know Him more with an intensity that yielded results. In the next chapter, I will show you how.

11
MORE ON JESUS AND THE HOLY SPIRIT

I would like to share with you in this chapter one of the encounters I had with Jesus that stands out in my mind, because it helped me overcome unbelief.

In a dream, I saw myself going towards a church. However, as I got close to the church building, I noticed what looked like a little shaft of light in the midst of a thick white cloud. I was puzzled about it and I began to enquire within myself about what I had seen, still staring intently at the light. Suddenly, the 'head' of a man slowly manifested itself through the beam of light and I asked tentatively, 'Who is this?' Just then, what had appeared as a human head began to turn gradually towards me and, as the 'head' was turning, a cloud began to unravel around him.

In an instant, I could see from His face to His waistline and He stretched His two hands up. Like a thunderbolt, the reality of the magnificence I beheld struck me and then I bellowed, 'This is Jesus!' It was so exhilarating that all I could do was stare at Jesus, even though what was on my mind was a lifelong desire for Him to empower me. I was so eager to ask Jesus to empower me and it was at the tip of my mouth to make the request, but no sound came out. My lips trembled so fiercely as I tried to ask Him to give me power, yet I couldn't utter a word. His Majesty, the Lord Jesus simply smiled at me. He had the smile on His face as He went back into the cloud in the same manner He had appeared, with the cloud twirling around him.

After he had departed, still in the dream I began to feel sorry for myself saying, 'Oh God, oh God, why couldn't I ask Him?' Then I walked into the church where there was a crusade going on and I joined in. In that crusade I saw some pastors who I eventually met later in real life. There was a minister who was preaching and asking people if they wanted to be baptised in the Holy Spirit. He said if anybody wanted to be baptised in the Holy Spirit he should fast for three days.

As I was praying in that dream, the Holy Ghost came upon me. My legs were lifted up about a foot above the ground and while I was floating I began speaking in tongues profusely. As I was enjoying this occurrence I woke up, startled to realise it had been a dream.

Before this time I had not been speaking in tongues and when I woke up from that encounter I wasn't speaking in tongues either. I wondered, 'Oh God, what is this? I have been asking to see You. Yet when you appeared to me I couldn't even ask You for power?' My heart pondered tirelessly on this and I became even more determined to walk in the ways of the Lord.

About two or three years after this dream, an evangelist visited my neighbourhood and conducted a three-day crusade, which I attended. On the first day the evangelist said, 'If you want to be baptised in the Holy Ghost you must fast and pray for three days.' Those interested, including myself, began the fast and on the third day, as we prayed, people got baptised in the Holy Ghost one by one.

While I was praying I asked God to baptise me with the Holy Ghost, but nothing happened. During the prayer, I poured my heart out to God, telling Him I had done everything that He had instructed me to do according to His word and that those who were receiving the Holy Ghost baptism were not as committed as I was in the church and neither were they as spiritually mature as I was. I even told the

> *I*mmediately, with a sudden jolt of awareness, I realised that the man I had seen in my dream was the one who was conducting the crusade!...

Lord that I attended church all the time and almost slept in the church, unlike many others who had simply come to church on the occasion of the crusade.

As I was praying, suddenly my memory flashed back and I recollected the dream I had three years earlier where I had seen myself being filled with the Holy Ghost. Immediately, with a sudden jolt of awareness, I realised that the man I had seen in my dream was the one who was conducting the crusade! I remembered the multitudes as they had been seated in the dream. It became clear to me that this was the incident God had revealed to me three years before! Ecstatically, I began expressing my heartfelt gratitude to God for the Holy Ghost and for baptising me already. Soon the encounter in the dream materialised in the natural! Suddenly, I became baptised in the Holy Ghost and lo and behold, my feet were lifted up about a foot from the ground. It was a moment in my life I will never forget. The man who was sitting beside me opened his eyes, and as he saw my feet suspended in mid air, he ran out of the church. The service nearly came to a stop as everyone stared at the man who stood in the air! What has God revealed to you that you are yet to see the materialisation of? If He said it, He will do it. Believe God, regardless of how long it may seem that you have not yet seen the manifestation of His revelation. God does not lie: this simple and mind-blowing fact, once grasped, will change your life for ever.

12

DREAMS

School days

When I was studying for one of my examinations at the Federal School of Surveying, the Lord Jesus appeared to me and took me to a classroom. He showed me the Mathematics level 4 examination papers and asked whether I could answer the questions therein. I said 'No', so He sat me down and explained what the questions meant and the answers to them by doing a mathematical analysis on the classroom writing board. When He finished, He asked whether I understood what he had just explained and as I answered 'Yes'. It seemed as though all the mathematical analysis He did on the board had entered my brain and I understood perfectly all that He had explained. I woke up at 3am the following morning and called my friend Pius.

I told Pius what I had seen in my encounter with Jesus, and he wrote down the questions as I described them. On arrival at the examination hall, we noted that the questions Jesus had shown me in my dream were accurate, word for word and figure for figure. Subsequently, Pius told all his friends about my dream and the examination papers. I always prayed every midnight hour and while I was praying the following night the entrance to the room was jammed with Pius's friends who had been told about my dream. They blocked the entrance to my room because they did not want anyone to disturb my sleep after having said my prayer. The Lord visited me again and revealed the next day's examination papers to me. I woke up about 3am to find some students waiting to see me; they asked, 'What did you see? What did you see?' I recounted it to them.

> *I* woke up about 3am to find some students waiting to see me; they asked, 'What did you see? What did you see?'...

At the examination hall, no one was disappointed. These encounters made my schoolmates show exceptional kindness to me. They looked at me as a mysterious being, but to me this was a normal life every Christian ought to have. There could be someone reading this who is wondering to himself whether Jesus was biased in showing me the examination papers, thus helping me to score 100% in those examinations. I would like to explain something simple but liberating to you: God has singled out some individuals over the ages and revealed himself to them while lavishing His grace upon them. God has sovereign choice which no man can begin to comprehend. The story of Bezalel and Oholiab is an example of one of such instances.

Exodus 31: 1-6

1 Then the LORD said to Moses, 2 "See, I have chosen Bezalel son of Uri, the son of Hur, of the tribe of Judah, 3 and I have filled him with the Spirit of God, with wisdom, with understanding, with knowledge and with all kinds of skills — 4 to make artistic designs for work in gold, silver and bronze, 5 to cut and set stones, to work in wood, and to engage in all kinds of crafts. 6 Moreover, I have appointed Oholiab son of Ahisamak, of the tribe of Dan, to help him. Also I have given ability to all the skilled workers to make everything I have commanded you...

Again, during a time of famine, another individual, a widow, in the bible experienced God's sovereign grace. Take a look at *2 Kings 4: 1-7:*

1 The wife of a man from the company of the prophets cried out to Elisha, "Your servant my husband is dead, and you know that he revered the LORD. But now his creditor is coming to take my two boys as his slaves." 2 Elisha replied to her, "How can I help you? Tell me, what do you have in your house?"

"Your servant has nothing there at all," she said, "except a small jar of olive oil." 3 Elisha said, "Go around and ask all your n eighbours for empty jars. Don't ask for just a few. 4 Then go inside and shut the door behind you and your sons. Pour oil into all the jars, and as each is filled, put it to one side." 5 She left him and shut the door behind her and her sons. They brought the jars to her and she kept pouring. 6 When all the jars were full, she said to her son, "Bring me another one." But he replied, "There is not a jar left." Then the oil stopped flowing. 7 She went and told the man of God, and he said, "Go, sell the oil and pay your debts. You and your sons can live on what is left."

Would you say God was biased in blessing this widow with such favour? He chose her to enjoy the beauty of His supernatural provision for financial increase. Why her and not her next door neighbor? Only God can answer that. When you choose to buy a gift for one friend and simply say happy birthday to another, no one can question your choice, because you have given from personal choice.

Another instance I would share with you is regarding a member of our Church who is now a pastor in London. He encountered one of such unique blessings from God in the area of his finances.

One day this man came to my house in a very distressed and confused state. After welcoming him, he sat down and wailed, ' Pastor my life is over! The bailiffs have come to clear my house and my office. ' He rested his head on his hands and wept bitterly. I simply allowed him to weep for a while, then when he stopped I asked him, 'are you through with weeping?' He replied, 'yes'.

Then I told him to stand up and let us pray. I quoted *Ephesians 2: 6* - which states that:

> 6 *And God raised us up with Christ and seated us with him in the heavenly realms in Christ Jesus,*

While we were praying, I saw both of us in heaven and other people in a place that appeared like a courtroom. The people were coming up one at a time to defend themselves against the accusations being presented by the devil, respectively. Then suddenly it was the brother's turn to defend himself and I stood up. Instantly, I saw Jesus walk into the room and He quoted several scriptures in defence of the man. And immediately, the person who appeared as the judge acquitted the brother as free – case dismissed!

I then asked the Lord about the brother's outstanding debts and Jesus said I should instruct him to go to a place called Wickford, which until then I had never heard of. Jesus told me to tell him to go to a bank there, that he had prepared money for him which he was to use to revive his business.

With that, I became conscious of my surroundings and I opened my eyes to see the brother sitting on my couch and watching me expectantly. Apparently, my prayers had taken on a different tone and he knew that I must be seeing something. Immediately I said, 'do you know a place called Wickford ?' At once he nodded excitedly and I continued, ' the Lord says go to the bank after the bridge there and collect the ten thousand pounds you need for your business'.

He looked at me bewildered. 'How can this happen, Sir, when I have been declared bankrupt? '

I told him, 'Jesus has made the provision, simply tell the bank manager that your pastor instructed you to go there'.

He finally got up and mustered the courage to go to the bank. When he got to the bank and said 'I want to see the manager'. The person at the reception said he could not see the manager without a prior appointment. He insisted that he had to see the manager. Finally, the manger came out and noticed their exchange and joined them asking him what he required. He told the manager that his pastor told him to come there to collect ten thousand pounds to revive his business. The manager invited him into his office and he explained the truth of his financial crisis and how he had a new order which entailed huge profits, but he had no cash to execute the order.

After the manager took all his details, he told him to go home and promised to come to see him on Thursday. The brother came away from the meeting still worried. And I pointed out to him that bank managers were too busy to pay visits to people if they did not plan to take matters one step further. I told him the manager would come with the money. And that was exactly what happened. The manager arrived on Thursday as promised and told him that normally, he was far from qualified for ten thousand pounds loan; however, he had opened a bank account for the brother with the overdraft facilities of ten thousand pounds! Within a couple of days, the brother was at the bank and was able to collect the money. This was how the brother was able to execute his business and overcome his financial problem at the time. Our God is an awesome God. He blesses as He chooses.

I have always been taught that whenever I find myself in dire straits, if I call to Jesus He will come swiftly to my aid. I called on Jesus; I suppose if my schoolmates had also called on Him, He would have come to their aid too. Furthermore, *Daniel 2: 19* states: "During the night the mystery was revealed to Daniel in a vision. Then Daniel praised the God of heaven and said: 'Praise be to the name of God for ever and ever; wisdom and power are his.' " Jesus is the giver and revealer of mystery and if Christians acquaint themselves with Him, through prayers, that is observing the hours of prayers and studying the word, then Jesus can help such Christians to gain a better understanding of any form of mystery in their lives.

The will of God is that all His children can encounter Him. Some Christians have bad dreams where evil spirits disturb their sleep. This ought not to be; Christians should not have bad dreams. If Satan's messengers can visit people in their sleep to destroy them, how much more can an angel visit a child of God? God gives visions of the night (dreams) as a medium of communication/interaction with Him. There are quite a few other members in my church who have also had visions from the Lord.

Get ready for God's visitation in your dream

God uses very individualistic language to communicate information to us while dreaming. He uses elements from our life journeys, our personal behaviours and biblical examples. God speaks to everyone through dreams in one way or another, but whether you are attuned to receive the message is a totally different matter. What your spirit does while you are asleep is controllable by you to a certain degree. *1 Corinthians 14: 32* states that: "The spirits of prophets are subject to the control of prophets." Unlike men, God does not show favouritism; therefore, if you expect His visitation, He will honour you with His presence.

Acts 10: 34–35 says:

"34 Then Peter began to speak: 'I now realise how true it is that God does not show favouritism, 35 but accepts from every nation the one who fears him and does what is right."

Different types of dreams

1. **There are false dreams, which arise as a fabricated delusion of the dreamer's heart.** *Jeremiah 23: 25–26* says:

"25 I have heard what the prophets say who prophesy lies in my name. They say, 'I had a dream! I had a dream!' 26 How long will this continue in the hearts of these lying prophets, who prophesy the delusions of their own minds?"

See also *Jeremiah 29: 8* (NKJ).

2. **There are true dreams. True dreams can be given by God for direction as follows:**

a.   Directional dreams: *Acts 16: 10*

b.   For encouragement: *Judges 7: 13–15*

c.   For warnings: *Job 33: 14–18*

d.   To reveal destiny: *Genesis 37: 5–11*

e.   For prophetic direction: *1 Samuel 28: 6*

3. **God can interact with man through dreams.** *Genesis 20: 1–7* says:

"1 Now Abraham moved on from there into the region of Negev and lived between Kadesh and Shur. For a while he stayed in Gerar, 2 and there Abraham said of his wife Sarah, 'She is my

sister.' Then Abimelek king of Gerar sent for Sarah and took her. 3 But God came to Abimelek in a dream one night and said to him, 'You are as good as dead because of the woman you have taken; she is a married woman.' 4 Now Abimelek had not gone near her, so he said, 'Lord, will you destroy an innocent nation? 5 Did he not say to me, "She is my sister," and didn't she also say, "He is my brother"? I have done this with a clear conscience and clean hands.' 6 Then God said to him in the dream, 'Yes, I know you did this with a clear conscience, and so I have kept you from sinning against me. That is why I did not let you touch her. 7 Now return the man's wife, for he is a prophet, and he will pray for you and you will live. But if you do not return her, you may be sure that you and all who belong to you will die.' "

4. **There are trances:** this is when you are in a state of part or complete detachment from your surroundings. They can occur anywhere and anytime. Trances make you feel as if you are in the grey area between sleep and awareness. *Acts 22: 17–18 says:*

"17 When I returned to Jerusalem and was praying at the temple, I fell into a trance 18 and saw the Lord speaking to me. 'Quick!' he said. 'Leave Jerusalem immediately, because the people here will not accept your testimony about me.'
See also *Acts 10: 9–10.*

Every dream is a deposit

Not remembering your dream is not necessarily a reason to cast away dreams, as every dream you have is a seed already deposited into your subconscious. In some instances, memories of these deposits are triggered by an event or by the Holy Spirit. Because God is depositing into your spirit during every dream encounter, you need to be expectant and ensure that your dream life is not left to negative influences. Solomon received divine wisdom in his dream; see *1 Kings 3: 5* (NIV):

> *"At Gibeon the LORD appeared to Solomon during the night in a dream, and God said, 'Ask for whatever you want me to give you.' "*

> *1 Kings 3:10–15* continues: *"10 The Lord was pleased that Solomon had asked for this. 11 So God said to him, 'Since you have asked for this and not for long life or wealth for yourself, nor have asked for the death of your enemies but for discernment in administering justice, 12 I will do what you have asked. I will give you a wise and discerning heart, so that there will never have been anyone like you, nor will there ever be. 13 Moreover, I will give you what you have not asked for –both wealth and honour – so that in your lifetime you will have no equal among kings. 14 And if you walk in obedience to me and keep my decrees and commands as David your father did, I will give you a long life.' 15 Then Solomon awoke – and he realised it had been a dream."*

If you read further on the life of Solomon, you will see that the blessing God bestowed on him in his dream came to fruition. It happened to Solomon, it has happened to me, so why not for you as well?

Steps to take upon waking up from a dream

1. Allow the peace of God to dominate your mind the instant you open your eyes. Make this a daily practice as long as you live.

2. Avoid speaking to people immediately you open your eyes and allow the contents of the dream to pour through your

awareness. Then take the few moments that are required for you to ask God about what you have seen in the dream.

3. Make an effort to go through every aspect of the encounter you have just experienced, and then put it in writing in order to refer back to it.

4. Prayer is the essential step to take before beginning your day. Pray concerning every part of the dream, including any part you do not understand. If you are puzzled by the dream, endeavour to narrate it to someone who is highly trusted in your life.

5. Remember that not all dreams must inevitably happen. Many dreams are warnings of possibilities while some are for enlightenment. You can make declarations regarding a dream where you are in disagreement with the content.

6. Whatever happens, do not cast away puzzling dreams. Make it a point of duty to ponder on them and treasure them until the appointed time. See, for example, *Genesis 37: 10–11:*

"10 When he told his father as well as his brothers, his father rebuked him and said, 'What is this dream you had? Will your mother and I and your brothers actually come and bow down to the ground before you?' 11 His brothers were jealous of him, but his father kept the matter in mind."

7. When your dream is a rebuke from God, you should avoid ignoring it. He loves you and every correction through your dream should be embraced with thanksgiving. Better to receive this correction in private and address it than to risk public disgrace

by Satan. *Psalm 32: 5* says:

"5 Then I acknowledged my sin to you and did not cover up my iniquity. I said, 'I will confess my transgressions to the LORD.' – and you forgave the guilt of my sin."

And *Habakkuk 2: 1* states:

"1 I will stand at my watch and station myself on the ramparts; I will look to see what he will say to me, and what answer I am to give to this complaint."

8.   If your dream is warning against something dangerous happening or circumstances that are revolutionary, then make every effort to be calm and not jump to hasty conclusions. *Daniel 4: 28–31* says:

"28 All this happened to King Nebuchadnezzar. 29 Twelve months later, as the king was walking on the roof of the royal palace of Babylon, 30 he said, 'Is not this the great Babylon I have built as the royal residence, by my mighty power and for the glory of my majesty?'

31 Even as the words were on his lips, a voice came from heaven, 'This is what is decreed for you, King Nebuchadnezzar: Your royal authority has been taken from you.' "

If you do not want to be a victim of repeated odd circumstances, you will take charge of every aspect of your life in order to encounter God in all the dimensions He has made available to man. In the next chapter, I would like to share another testimony of God's revelation to me and how it came to pass.

APOSTLE ALFRED TB WILLIAMS

What can hinder you from receiving Godly (true) dreams?

1. Getting drunk with alcohol or getting high on hard drugs – *Isaiah 29: 9–11*

2. Lack of peace in your soul

3. Grieving the Holy Spirit – *Ephesians 4: 29–32*

"29 Do not let any unwholesome talk come out of your mouths, but only what is helpful for building others up according to their needs, that it may benefit those who listen. 30 And do not grieve the Holy Spirit of God, with whom you were sealed for the day of redemption. 31 Get rid of all bitterness, rage and anger, brawling and slander, along with every form of malice. 32 Be kind and compassionate to one another, forgiving each other, just as in Christ God forgave you.

4. Pride

"5 The LORD detests all the proud of heart. Be sure of this: They will not go unpunished."

5. Walking in unforgiveness

6. Taking the word of the Lord for granted

7. Anything that can cause you to lose self-control

8. Watching unedifying films and dramas or plays

A lot of people panic when shown revelations about things to happen. Imagine if I had panicked when the Lord told me about September 11 or other major incidents? How would I have been able to enter the place of thanksgiving and make use of the opportunity to pray concerning the people or the event?

If you do not want to be a victim of repeated odd circumstances, you will take charge of every aspect of your life in order to encounter God in all the dimensions He has made available to man. In the next chapter, I would like to share another testimony of God's revelation to me and how it came to pass.

13

THE RECORD ROOM

Marriage

For a very long time after I proposed to my wife, my father-in-law refused to give her hand to me in marriage, even though every other member of her family including her mother was very excited at the prospect of me becoming their in-law. His reason was that he did not want someone from another tribe marrying his precious daughter. He had hoped and convinced himself that she would definitely marry from his own tribe. We prayed and prayed for four years and pleaded with him. We bought the first wedding gown in 1979, and one of our friends got married in it; we bought the second wedding gown in 1980, and another one of our friends wore that for their wedding; we went ahead again and bought the third wedding gown in 1981, and the same thing happened. We thought we were acting by faith not recognising the difference between the two.

I decided to seek the face of the Lord earnestly concerning the matter, as it was impossible for me to marry her without her father's consent or blessing. That was the way we were brought up. I started praying and seeking His face and after some time the Lord took me into a place in heaven and showed me the calendar of months. When He opened the calendar, it was like a moving picture (a video). He began to open it from the day I started praying till April 1983. He told me that was the month of my marriage and that I should choose a day. I said to the Lord the 30th of that month. He replied 'You got it right' and I was happy that I had got it right in His presence. But He spoke again and said, 'No one gets it wrong in My presence.' He also told me that I had chosen right and He showed me the 30th of that month, and how the marriage would be from the church service to the reception at the end.

Therefore, from 1981 we stopped buying wedding gowns and we then waited until 1983. We printed the wedding cards and made all the preparations for the day and two weeks before the wedding my father-in-law accepted me. That was how our marriage came about. To this day my wife has been a tremendous blessing and is extremely helpful in supporting me in the fulfilment of God's mandate upon my life. She is very understanding, though we have our personal human unique differences and sometimes we have to work things out. Her ministry has indeed been of a tremendous support.

14

THE THRONE ROOM

*T*he first time I visited the throne room was in 1998, when the Lord took me to a room where God takes decisions over nations. *Daniel 7: 9–10* describes this great room thus:

> *"9 As I looked, thrones were set in place, and the Ancient of Days took his seat. His clothing was as white as snow; the hair of his head was white like wool. His throne was flaming with fire, and its wheels were all ablaze. 10 A river of fire was flowing, coming out from before him. Thousands upon thousands attended him; ten thousand times ten thousand stood before him. The court was seated, and the books were opened."*

An angel appeared to me in my dream and I went out of my body and landed in the presence of angels ministering to the Almighty Father. It was here, in the throne room, that He revealed the outcome of the political unrest in an African nation in that year. In that encounter, I heard the Lord say to an angel, 'Go now and take out that man; the cup of his iniquity is full' and, instantaneously, the presidential lodge of an African president appeared to us in full view and I saw an angel moving towards the president as he walked down the stairs in the lodge. When he got to the second to last step of the staircase, the angel placed a finger on the president's forehead and he slumped to the floor, dead. The angel came back to the throne room and said, 'It is done.' The Father then turned to me and said, 'Go now and tell my people in that nation to stop praying to me about their country, for I have risen for the cause, of the nation and on the 7th of July

> He spoke to me about the 9/11 disaster which occurred in 2001. Just a day before the tragedy, I was...

this same year, they will see my hands again in that nation.' He also said I should caution anyone who tried to stand against his purpose for the nation. Needless to say, the president's death sparked a lot of rumours within and outside the borders of that nation. But I know it was the Lord Almighty who put an end to his lifespan.

In the latter part of 1999, when the fear about the millennium bug was spreading like wildfire among some of my ministerial contemporaries, I went to the Lord in prayer asking about what would happen in the new millennium. Subsequently, the Lord took me to a place in heaven, where the calendar of this world is kept. Although they look like calendars, they are in fact diaries. In each diary lies the activities of each day, each year and each season. This gave me an understanding that God truly is an all-knowing God. Although He knows everything that will happen, nevertheless, He does not orchestrate the disasters on earth and rarely ever interferes in the affairs of mankind. It was while in His presence in that encounter that He spoke to me about the 9/11 disaster which occurred in 2001. Just a day before the tragedy, I was preaching at one of the Christ Apostolic Church (CAC) churches in Leyton, when the Spirit of the Lord reminded me of the vision that the Lord had shown me in 1999, concerning some of the incidents that would occur on earth between the years 2000 and 2015. He then informed me that one of those incidents would occur in the USA, the next day about noon. I announced this to all the pastors and members of the congregation present in that meeting. I told them of a great tragedy that would befall America the next day, which would have devastating consequences on the world economy. I returned to our headquarters church and related this information to my members. I also wrote to some of my American counterparts about what the Lord had said, urging them not to be afraid about the millennium bug for it would most certainly not occur.

During that same encounter in 1999, the Lord also showed me the nation of Cote d'Ivoire. I also told them the Lord had said that if anyone doubted what He had revealed to me, I should tell them that within a very short space of time a nation that knew no war would be plunged into one. He mentioned that Cote d'Ivoire would experience a bloodless coup which would ultimately result in a war.

In the realm of the spirit one can be given a volume of information that spans decades in the twinkling of an eye. It is possible to see everything that will happen on a daily basis in the next ten years, but when you come out from that encounter you are not able to remember everything until the time that the incidents are due to occur. The testimonies I am sharing with you are not an abstract expression of my thoughts or imagination. They are real occurrences that time has proven, and will continue to prove, to be true.

Revelations about recession and famine in Europe

A couple of years ago while worshipping in our London church, I was caught up in the Spirit of the Lord and saw that in and around the borders of Europe were drought and famine. This was not like the famine of Africa where terrible droughts occur. But in this encounter I saw that although there were water shortages, the main dilemma of the nations was starvation. The cost of basic food items skyrocketed to the extent that even the very wealthy felt the squeeze. It is no surprise to me that people are beginning to complain about the cost of living. It is equally not surprising that some countries in Europe are in a deep recession.

In Britain, as news about the recession began to hit our high streets resulting in some companies folding up and subsequent huge rises in unemployment, the Lord visited me and told me that in two weeks' time the stock exchange would crash, which I announced to the church.

One of my spiritual sons, who works as a senior banker in the City, heard about this and shared this information with his colleagues. They all mocked him, saying that he was speaking the impossible as all economic analytical forecasts at the time predicted the opposite. Nevertheless, a day before the predicted crash, he sold off all his shares. The majority of them were purchased by his friends, who did not believe his revelation and kept on reiterating that he was going 'bonkers'. Not long thereafter, a shock wave swept through the stock market as share prices began to plunge. Some weeks afterwards, the Lord told me that He had given Gordon Brown, then UK prime minister, the wisdom to solve the world economic crash. I wrote to Gordon Brown at the time about God's prophecy. The economy will recover between April and August.

It was also during this period that the Lord visited me again and took me to a classroom and showed me the economic graph of the world. He told me that a part of the graph has two sides. One part of it is called the actual graph while the other part is called the virtual graph. He explained that when human beings build their economy on virtual assets, the graph goes upwards until it reaches the maximum turnover and then begins to drop and drop below the actual graph. It continues dropping until it reaches the below-zero margin. Those who build their economy on virtual assets which do not exist are the ones who will suffer. But those who build their economy on the actual graph will survive the economy.

For the Lord had told me about the G12 and G20 meetings in March and April respectively. He said that after those meetings there would be a recovery in the stock market, especially with Barclays stocks. I urged all my church members to purchase shares in Barclays Bank. Some of our members profited from my prophecy about the state of the economy, here in the UK.

2 Kings 7: 1 confirms that this sort of vision can occur in the life of a believer. It reads thus: "Then Elisha said, 'Listen to the word of the LORD; thus says the LORD, "Tomorrow about this time a measure of fine flour will be sold for a shekel, and two measures of barley for a shekel, in the gate of Samaria." ' " My prayer is that the verse 3 of that scripture will not be the portion of anyone reading this scripture. Neither do you need to panic about the present economic climate, as God's promises for His saints states that in times of famine, we will have plenty *(Psalm 37: 19)*.

15

THE AUDIBLE VOICE

*T*here is no such thing in the Bible as the gift of vision, trance or hearing the audible voice of God. There is also nothing like the gift of revelation in the scriptures. What then is revelation?, you may ask. This is an atmosphere where God sends an angel to a person in broad daylight and gives that person a message that is divine. The angel will tell of things that are yet to happen or things that have already taken place and the solutions to them. That is a form of heavenly revelation.

Open vision

When a person is experiencing an open vision, that person becomes unconscious of their earthly realm but has a full consciousness of the spiritual realm where the vision is being given. That person has a clear and distinct vision of the activities going on in that encounter, which is why when a person has had an open vision they never forget what occurred therein. An open vision occurs when a person is physically awake, either in the midst of people or by themselves. Often, it happens suddenly, in a split second, as though one is watching a television screen. You will be totally captivated by that scene and oblivious to everything else in the world during that encounter. Open vision is not an imagination of the mind. It is a manifestation of reality that can be seen but through a person's spiritual eyes, which in all cases have a clearer view than mankind's natural physical eyesight. See *Acts 10: 3–7*.

Trance

However, in a trance, a person becomes semi-conscious of their environment (say about 20% consciousness in the physical realm but 80% consciousness or alertness in the spiritual realm) such that when they speak, their speech becomes slurred causing them to be unable to fully communicate with their intelligence within the physical realm. That person will hear conversations around them in both realms, but will have a better understanding and alertness and be more active in the spiritual realm than the physical realm. The major difference between a trance and a vision is that in a vision one completely loses one's physical senses and concentration is purely in the spiritual realm, but with a trance one still has a bit of both spiritual and natural consciousness. See *Acts 10: 9–23*.

There is also the audible voice of God, where God speaks to a person in an audible voice. If in the company of people, there are two ways God does this. Sometimes He allows others around to hear a rumbling (see *1 Samuel 3: 1– 10; Acts 9: 3–7*). At other times He allows them to hear a part of what He's saying but the very man that God is speaking to, from the first discussion to the last discussion, will hear God distinctly and clearly. An audible voice comes in various streams or spiritual waves of frequencies. Sometimes it sounds as though you are hearing a still voice from a far distance similar to an echo. God speaks like that and at other times it seems like someone has put their mouth close to your ears and is speaking into your ears, but when you turn around to see the person whose voice you have heard, they are nowhere close to you. There are other times when it appears as though someone walking around you is speaking in a loud familiar voice. When you look around the person the sound of whose f voice you have heard is nowhere close to you: this is God speaking.

We must note, however, that an audible voice, trance or vision are not gifts from God but are manifestations that come upon a person because of their relationship with God. The more intimate you become with God through acts of righteousness and of course the disciplines of praying, reading the scriptures and fasting, as you are led to, you get closer and closer and closer to the reality of God. This grace begins to occur in such a person's life.

Another means by which God speaks to people is through dreams or revelations of the night. The difference between a vision of the night, which is a dream given by God, and a normal dream is this: when you have a normal dream, most times when you wake up you forget the details. When God gives you a dream/revelation, when you wake up you never forget the details. Additionally, when God gives you a vision or a dream, if you don't act on the vision, God will revisit you and repeat the same vision, to confirm that He is the one speaking to you.

It is worth stating here that just as God uses angels in dreams to communicate messages, so too does Satan use demons to infiltrate people. The ultimate goal for believers while sleeping is to have a consciousness of what happens in their dreams. If a

Christian is not conscious in their dream, then Satan will sometimes visit their dreams to oppress them. There are some Christians who eat in their dreams and when they wake up they panic. You don't have to panic. Some of you have been misled into thinking that because you ate in the dream you have to run from pillar to post seeking deliverance. You don't need to do that. If you eat in your dream, it is because you have not understood what your spiritual exercise is, and have lost your guard. Your spiritual exercise entails developing your mind by the word of God and loving the Lord your God with all your heart and committing yourself to prayer and studying the Bible.

> *S*ome of our members profited from my prophecy about the state of the economy, here in the UK...

It is what occupies your mind that determines what can enter into your dream, and whenever evil infiltrates your dream Satan can beat you up in your dream or chase you all over the place. At the end of it you call on Jesus, and Jesus will not come out at the time you wanted him to come out but, whatever the case may be, the Lord Jesus was there to help you anyway, and eventually you wake up and say, 'Thank God I'm up.' It doesn't matter whether you ate on your dream or you are sexually abused in your dream. The Bible says you will eat deadly poison, but it will not harm you.

It didn't say you will eat deadly poison when you're awake. Whether you're awake or you're asleep, it will not harm you. When you wake up, put your hands on that tummy and say, 'Bless the Lord, Oh my soul and ALL that's within me, praise His Holy Name', and move on. Don't ever for, whatever reason, begin to get worried that something bad will happen to you because of the negative or bad dreams you had – especially if you have made Jesus Christ your Lord and Saviour. The reason why many Christians appear to be physically affected by their dreams is because of their mindset. Yet a Christian is fully capable of developing their mind to a place where in the dream they can easily challenge any authority. I am compiling a series on the interpretations of dreams and visions; anyone who wants to know more can place an order for it, and in the interim my teachings on dreams and interpretations are available on CDs/DVD from our church office.

16

HOW CAN MORTAL MAN ATTAIN THIS LEVEL OF EXPERIENCE WITH GOD?

*I*f you profess to be a Christian who regularly attends church services and functions yet you live a life that is void of Christian ethics as written in the scriptures, I am sorry to inform you that should death meet you living in that frame of mind, you are going to hell and there is no substitute for hell. Jesus said that not everyone who calls Him Lord will enter the kingdom of His Father *(Matthew 7: 21, 1 Corinthians 6: 9–10, Ephesians 5: 5–7)*.

You may be wondering how we know those who are truly born again, since we are not God who can read the hearts of mankind and know what people get up to in their closets. The answer is this: first by their fruits you will know them *(Matthew 7: 16)*. A Christian is someone who has not only accepted Jesus Christ as their personal Lord and Saviour but who has also stopped living according to the sinful nature, because the Spirit of Christ in them convicts them of sin. If, for instance, before you became a Christian you loved going to clubhouses and partying all night long, week in week out, the moment you get born again you will instantaneously hate such a lifestyle, because the Spirit of God which now dwells in you will convict you about living that sort of life. The law of conscience is an imprint of the Spirit of God in a person. Evidence of the indwelling Spirit of God in you is a constant conviction of evil in your heart. The church can only give you the knowledge of what the Lord will not permit you to do, but it is only the Holy Spirit that can convict a person's heart of evil. When a person genuinely follows the precepts of God, even though physically that person may struggle, within their inner man (heart) they will have peace. *Romans 8: 1–9* explains it better:

"Therefore, there is now no condemnation for those who are in Christ Jesus, 2 because through Christ Jesus the law of the Spirit who gives life has set you free from the law of sin and death. 3 For what the law was powerless to do because it was weakened by the flesh, God did by sending his own Son in the likeness of sinful flesh to be a sin offering. And so he condemned sin in the flesh, 4 in order that the righteous requirement of the law might be fully met in us, who do not live according to the flesh but according to the Spirit. 5 Those who live according to the flesh have their minds set on what the flesh desires; but those who live in accordance with the Spirit have their minds set on what the Spirit desires. 6 The mind governed by the flesh is death, but the mind governed by the Spirit is life and peace. 7 The mind governed by the flesh is hostile to God; it does not submit to God's law, nor can it do so. 8 Those who are in the realm of the flesh cannot please God. 9 You, however, are not in the realm of the flesh but are in the realm of the Spirit, if indeed the Spirit of God lives in you. And if anyone does not have the Spirit of Christ, they do not belong to Christ."

So why then do some Christians get frustrated, if the Holy Spirit is there for us all? Why are they not able to receive directions from the Holy Spirit? I strongly believe it is because there is a rule for the Holy Spirit. If you call Him Holy, you as His temple cannot be unholy. If you want to see through the eyes of the Holy Spirit, it cannot be through the eyes of an adulterer or fornicator. If you want the Holy Spirit to use you, you cannot engage yourself in the seven things the Lord hates as in *Proverbs 6:16–19* (NIV):

> *"16 There are six things the Lord hates, seven that are detestable to Him: 17 haughty eyes, a lying tongue, hands that shed innocent blood, 18 a heart that devises wicked schemes, feet that are quick to rush to evil, 19 a false witness who pours out lies and a man who stirs up dissension among brothers".*

You cannot operate in any or all of the acts above and expect the Holy Spirit to operate in holiness through you. This is the major problem for believers on earth and a problem that the present-day churches need to address urgently for the sake of those who wish to hear and listen to the truth (see *John 16: 7, 10*)

Here are some other scriptural references.

Ephesians 5: 3–7:

> *"3 But among you there must not be even a hint of sexual immorality, or of any kind of impurity, or of greed, because these are improper for God's holy people. 4 Nor should there be obscenity, foolish talk or coarse joking, which are out of place, but rather thanksgiving. 5 For of this you can be sure: No immoral, impure or greedy person – such a person is an idolater – has any inheritance in the kingdom of Christ and of God. 6 Let no one deceive you with empty words, for because of such things God's wrath comes on those who are disobedient. 7 Therefore do not be partners with them."*

Romans 12: 1–2:

"1Therefore, I urge you, brothers and sisters, in view of God's mercy, to offer your bodies as a living sacrifice, holy and pleasing to God – this is your true and proper worship. 2 Do not conform to the pattern of this world, but be transformed by the renewing of your mind. Then you will be able to test and approve what God's will is – his good, pleasing and perfect will."

There are people who say that their upbringing and background cause them to struggle with the reality of being a Christian as they have never been taught or brought up to adhere to certain Christian moral standards and thus struggle. Nevertheless, the truth is this: once you get born again and the Holy Spirit comes into you, which is evidence that you are born again, you don't need to know the ethics of Christianity because the Holy Spirit reveals all truth. The church can only give you knowledge out of the scriptures but it's the Holy Spirit that can stop a murderer from killing people, a thief from stealing, etc. (see *2 Corinthians 5: 17*). Therefore, whatever your parents used to be or taught you cannot be transferred, so why don't you commit yourself to the prayer of forgiveness?

Satan is always after the church and is happy to deceive people into going to hell. These days he does this by propagating prosperity and deliverance messages and many Christians still fall for his deception. There are parts in the Bible that are subject to human interpretation but there are also other parts that are clear and undebatable. For example, 'do not murder', 'do not commit adultery' and 'do not fornicate' are all clear and straightforward. It is only those who have made up their minds to go to hell that struggle with accepting this statement as true.

If we look again at the scripture in *John 14:18*, "I will not leave you as orphans...", that scripture tells me that the Holy Spirit was introduced by Jesus Christ to be our father. While Jesus Christ was on earth, He was a father to the disciples and if they needed anything they went to Him. Now when Jesus Christ was going, He said that He would give them the Holy Spirit so that they would not be made orphans by His departure. Even though He will die they will not be orphans, because He will send a Counsellor who will take over His role as a father so that before they do anything in life they can always go to Him and He will make sure that He guides them.

Now to give us a fuller confidence, Jesus went further in *John 16: 14–15* (NIV):

"14 He will bring glory to me by taking from what is mine and making it known to you. 15 All that belongs to the Father is mine. That is why I said the Spirit will take from what is mine and make it known to you."

Jesus declares here that He is going but we should not feel that He is deserting us because He will send the Holy Spirit who will father us and in order for us to have full confidence this Holy Spirit that He is sending has a duty to show us everything that belongs to Him. He also said that everything that belongs to the Father is His, which means that Jesus is saying directly to us that the Holy Spirit is the administrator that He has left to administer to us everything that God has prepared for our lives.

Once we acquaint ourselves with the Holy Spirit and follow His instructions and directions diligently, we too, in no time, will have easy access into the spiritual: realms where revelations, insights and knowledge (both fore- and pre-knowledge) can be easily accessible. That's how a mortal man can attain encounters of heaven.

17

HOW MUCH DO YOU LOVE GOD?

 ohn 5: 19–20 (NIV) says:

"Very truly I tell you, the Son can do nothing by himself; he can do only what he sees his Father doing, because whatever the Father does the Son also does. 20 For the Father loves the Son and shows him all he does. Yes, and he will show him even greater works than these, so that you will be amazed. 21 For just as the Father raises the dead and gives them life, even so the Son gives life to whom he is pleased to give it. 22 Moreover, the Father judges no one, but has entrusted all judgment to the Son, 23 that all may honour the Son just as they honour the Father. Whoever does not honour the Son does not honour the Father, who sent him."

Jesus only does what He sees His Father doing. The love of the Father determines how much of Himself He can reveal to you. I am not talking about agape love for salvation, which is the love God has for everyone thus sending His Son as redemption for our sins. However, when it comes to relationship, which is another level of love, then the love of God differs from one person to the other and this is dependent on how much of your heart, time and efforts you give to Him.

Why does the Father love the Son? According to *John 10: 17–18*:

*"17 The reason my Father loves me is that I lay down my life –
only to take it up again. 18 No one takes it from me, but I lay it
down of my own accord. I have authority to lay it down and
authority to take it up again. This command I received from
my Father."*

The Father loves the Son because He laid down His life in
complete obedience to die on the cross.

What can we do to show our love for God? *1 John 3: 16–18* says:

*"16This is how we know what love is: Jesus Christ laid down his
life for us. And we ought to lay down our lives for our brothers
and sisters. 17 If anyone has material possessions and sees a
brother or sister in need but has no pity on them, how can the
love of God be in that person? 18 Dear children, let us not love
with words or speech but with actions and in truth."*

This describes man's love for God. We ought to lay down
our lives for our brothers, and use practical means of expressing
love such as giving, sharing and helping. God loves everybody
but He is not able to reach anyone except through you, but as a
Christian if we fill the gap by meeting the needs of others around
us then we are expressing our love for God by helping Him to
reach His unreachable.

A total surrender and submission to God is also a form of
love. *1 John 1: 6* says: *"If we claim to have fellowship with him and yet
walk in the darkness, we lie and do not live out the truth."*

And *1 John 2: 3–6* says:

"3 We know that we have come to know him if we keep his commands. 4 Whoever says, 'I know him,' but does not do what he commands is a liar, and the truth is not in that person. 5 But if anyone obeys his word, love for God is truly made complete in them. This is how we know we are in him: 6 whoever claims to live in him must live as Jesus did."

And furthermore, 1 John 2: 9–10 says:

"9 Anyone who claims to be in the light but hates a brother or sister is still in the darkness. 10 Anyone who loves their brother and sister lives in the light, and there is nothing in them to make them stumble. 11 But anyone who hates a brother or sister is in the darkness and walks around in the darkness. They do not know where they are going, because the darkness has blinded them."

Jesus wants to show Himself to you but how much love do you have for Him in your heart? Do you still struggle with the things of this world? The only way a Christian can show he loves God is to obey the word. For whenever you obey the word of God you become the answer to many people's prayer. Salvation is not what many people think it is; it is deeper than just confessions but must be practical and full of good deeds.

Let me tell you something about this world. If you desire to have money, once you become wealthy you soon discover that every level of wealth comes with its own level of responsibility attached to it. These responsibilities will stretch your finances and level of tolerance to the limit. It is difficult to find a wealthy person who also has huge sums of savings in their bank account. Ask the big corporations who have huge investments; many of them also have huge debts. Look closely at everything in the world that captivates your attention. For example if you desire a husband or a wife, once you get one, you soon subconsciously instigate the problems associated with sharing a home life with a person of different characteristics, even though you may be in love. If you desire to have children, once they arrive you lose your independence as your life will thereafter revolve around them. You have to reduce your working and social hours to make time for them.

Hence all desires on earth come with their own troubles which mankind has adopted as part of the inevitable circumstances of life. No wonder Solomon states in *Ecclesiastes 12: 8:*

"8 Vanity of vanities, says the preacher; all is vanity."

But I can confidently inform you that the only aspect of one's life that cannot be classed as vanity is our love for God. God is willing to reveal Himself to you but are you willing to see Him?

If you are willing to see Him then you must love Him, and if you love Him then you must keep His commandments. Everything the Bible tells you not to do is for your own good. God is still God whether you obey Him or disobey Him: it does not change God in any form or shape. He has so many people who are seeking to obey Him; if you choose not to obey God, it is to your own peril. It does not change Him. Having academically and otherwise tried various spheres of life, I have come to discover, like King Solomon, that all is vanity upon vanity, I have come to the conclusion that the only worthwhile substance in life is for a mortal man to possess the ability to foretell the future – to have knowledge of what will occur in the days or weeks ahead – or to have the ability to travel back in time – on meeting people who are confused to be able to look at the archives of their lives as collated by God, in order to understand where they've gone wrong and tell them what to do to get back on track. I have seen people who are miserable, but having met with them and counselled them as directed by the Holy Spirit, I have seen a positive transformation in their lives in a matter of weeks or months.

I believe these offer a greater fulfilment in life. But you cannot attain this height without Jesus Christ revealing Himself to you. If you have been living in hurt, in rage, in lies or in deception, I tell you that you have no right to give yourself unnecessary problems. This is a wake-up call for repentance. You have no right to have high blood pressure that God did not give you, because of your attitude. Remember that you may not be able determine what life will throw at you but you most certainly have the right to determine how you will react in any given situation.

Lastly, remember that you may not be able to determine what life will throw at you but you most certainly have the right to determine how you will react in any given situation.

God bless you.

PRAYER

My God and Father, I thank you for those who have read this book. May your Holy Spirit grant them greater understanding than the words written in this book can convey.

Bring the hearts of those who are yet to know You to the place of repentance. May they forsake their ungodly ways and submit to your righteous living, so your name may be glorified in their lives. Father unto You immortal, invisible; unto You the only wise God, the one who was, is, and is to come.,the great I AM; unto You be the glory and honour and praise for ever and ever.

PRAYER OF SALVATION

Dear Jesus,

I acknowledge that you and the father are one
I come to you today with all of my heart.
I accept you as my personal Lord and Saviour
for you are the Son of God and no man cometh to
the Father except through you.

Cleanse my heart, O Lord and forgive
me for all my sins.
I surrender my spirit soul and body unto you and
receive you as my Lord and saviour.
Thank you, for I know you are now living in me.
In Jesus name, I have prayed.
Amen.

MY ENCOUNTERS WITH JESUS AND HIS ANGELS

Coming Soon

by Apostle A.T.B Williams

For more information contact:

email: info@revivalhousepublishing.com

124

Other titles
by Apostle A.T.B Williams

The Biblical instruction, teaching and guidance contained in this publication gives a theological framework to the role of a Shepherd that forms an apostolic teaching on the subject that is much needed, in our time. This apostolic teaching has not been formed in the calm interior of some remote seminary college, but rather, in the crucible of experience as the gospel has advanced forcibly amidst the resistance of the god of this age.

Order Hot-line 020 8133 9362

email: info@revivalhousepublishing.com
www.revivalhousepublishing.com

APOSTLE ALFRED TB WILLIAMS

APOSTLE ALFRED TB WILLIAMS